FAY THOMPSON

AZEZ MEDICINE

BALBOA
PRESS
A DIVISION OF HAY HOUSE

Copyright © 2013 Fay Thompson.

All rights reserved. No part of this book may be used or reproduced by any means, graphic, electronic, or mechanical, including photocopying, recording, taping or by any information storage retrieval system without the written permission of the publisher except in the case of brief quotations embodied in critical articles and reviews.

Balboa Press books may be ordered through booksellers or by contacting:

Balboa Press
A Division of Hay House
1663 Liberty Drive
Bloomington, IN 47403
www.balboapress.com
1-(877) 407-4847

Because of the dynamic nature of the Internet, any web addresses or links contained in this book may have changed since publication and may no longer be valid. The views expressed in this work are solely those of the author and do not necessarily reflect the views of the publisher, and the publisher hereby disclaims any responsibility for them.

The author of this book does not dispense medical advice or prescribe the use of any technique as a form of treatment for physical, emotional, or medical problems without the advice of a physician, either directly or indirectly. The intent of the author is only to offer information of a general nature to help you in your quest for emotional and spiritual well-being. In the event you use any of the information in this book for yourself, which is your constitutional right, the author and the publisher assume no responsibility for your actions.

Any people depicted in stock imagery provided by Thinkstock are models, and such images are being used for illustrative purposes only.
Certain stock imagery © Thinkstock.

Printed in the United States of America

ISBN: 978-1-4525-6963-5 (sc)
ISBN: 978-1-4525-6965-9 (hc)
ISBN: 978-1-4525-6964-2 (e)

Library of Congress Control Number: 2013903963

Balboa Press rev. date: 3/20/2013

I dedicate this book to my darling husband Richard.
Thank you for believing in me.

CHAPTER 1

Meeting The Beings of the Light

"A star shone at the hour of our meeting." – JRR Tolkein

In November 2006, I attended my first spiritual weekend workshop. Up to that point, I knew very little about spiritual concepts. This weekend turned out to be a very pivotal moment in my life. It opened me to exploring the world of spirituality.

Once I found this world, I couldn't get enough of it. I read book after book. I scoured the Internet reading blogs and channels from various people. I attended several workshops, much to the annoyance of my husband who would often ask, "When are you going to find what you're searching for?"

I hadn't realized it at the time, but I had found what I was searching for. I had found spirituality. As I look back on what is a relatively short period of time, it is amazing to me how quickly things have come together. Within that time frame, I found my passion, opened to my intuitive abilities, took a leap of faith, quit my well-paying corporate job, became a Licensed Spiritual Health Coach, started my own business, created my own modality called Subconscious Mind Correction, began teaching spiritual workshops, and now have written a spiritual book. All of this would not have been possible if I hadn't taken that first workshop.

One of the areas of spirituality that always intrigued me was channeling. I had read several channeled books including ones by Sanaya Roman, Esther Hicks, and Lee Carroll. The information within these books resonated with me and I dreamed of how wonderful it would be to have instant access to an infinite source of wisdom as these channels had. How easy life would be!

Undaunted by the fact I had no idea what I was doing, I tried my hand at channeling. I did find a voice to listen to. I listened to this voice religiously for a couple of weeks. It told me how amazing my life was going to be and that I was going to do important work and be famous. It told me what I was doing wrong and pointed out exactly how I should be doing things. It even would interrupt me in my daily activities needing me to listen to it. Finally, it came to a point where I realized this was not the voice of a divine light being, but one that was out to make a fool of me.

Little did I know at the time it was merely the voice of my own ego. I thought I had been talking to something separate from myself. I actually became very scared, thinking I had tapped into some evil energy that may have attached itself to me, or worse, may try to possess me! I sought out the help of friends who were energy workers. They assured me I had no entities attached to me and that I was fine.

I gave up all attempts at channeling, until I saw an ad for a new workshop coming to town. It was called "Learning to Channel" taught by Pepper Lewis, who is well-known and well-respected in spiritual circles as the person who channels the energy of Gaia (Mother Earth).

Pepper taught me how to open my heart and mind and tap into the divine consciousness. She alleviated my fears regarding tapping into a dark energy. From this workshop, I learned that there is no hell, no Satan, and no evil. There is only the Source of unconditional love and our disconnection from it. When we disconnect from our Source of unconditional love, also known as our divinity, it feels like we are in hell, but we're not. The disconnection is nothing more than the experience of our ego, our place of fear, which is also the place from which all suffering comes. I had tapped into the dark when I first attempted channeling, but it was my own dark! It always is your own dark.

I also learned how to recognize whether one is tapped into the divine love Source or tapped into ego. Divine guidance is loving, accepting, and never judgmental. Divine guidance accepts you for what you have done and provides loving, action-based options to move you in the direction of a solution. Divine guidance doesn't tell you what you should do, but instead gives suggestions of what you could decide in order to make things better for yourself and others. Connection to divine guidance feels loving, supportive, and safe. When speaking directly with divine guidance, it will refer to itself as "we", instead of "I", because divine guidance understands the collective "We are all One", and doesn't separate itself as an individual like the ego does. Divine guidance offers love and hope, and never will add to your fear.

Ego, on the other hand, will judge you, tell you what you should or should not do, and make you feel guilty. Ego will inflate you to believe you are better than others and deflate you by saying, "Who are you to think you're so special?" Ego will stomp on others if it feels threatened, instead of seeking the truth. Ego will tell you if you need to be punished or if you need to suffer. Ego does not want you to be honest with your feelings, but instead hide from them. Ego will want to make decisions for you, instead of allowing you to make the best choice for yourself. Ego will tell you that you can't and make you afraid to act. An ego voice will refer to itself as "I" or "me", because it doesn't understand that we are One in love.

Learning the difference between divine guidance and the controlling ego made me realize even further the voice I "channeled" was indeed my own ego and not some evil trickster energy out to get me.

I also learned that channeled divine information can be expressed in a number of ways. It can come through your pen in written form through a process called automatic writing. It can come to you telepathically as intuitive guidance. It also can come through your speaking voice, where the channel allows the guidance to speak through them. The person (the channel) is not actually speaking, but instead they are allowing the guidance to be spoken through them from their own voice.

We practiced all these forms of channeling in the workshop. By actively participating in a variety of exercises, I realized there was nothing more to fear. I also realized that I had an aptitude for channeling. I seemed to be able to access a flow of divine information much more easily than many of the other workshop participants.

The night after the workshop ended, I sat in bed and decided to try channeling via the automatic writing method. Since I didn't know who I wanted to receive guidance from, I asked a generic question by stating with intent, "In the name of the light, whatever source of guidance that would be most beneficial for me to talk to, please make yourself known, and let me know what I most need to know for my highest good and the highest good of all involved."

I began to write. A stream of loving, kind information asking me to believe in myself and to follow my passion came through. It told me that whatever I needed to know, I need only ask, and the answer would be given. I knew this wasn't my ego talking. It sounded different in my head. Its voice was softer, kinder, and very loving. When I asked the source of this information to identify itself, it wrote on the page, "We are The Beings of the Light."

At that moment in time, I didn't think much about this group that I had just interacted with. I knew they were from the light and that was good enough for me. I went to bed feeling content.

As days passed, I continued the automatic writing sessions. Almost always, when I didn't specify the light source that I wished to contact, it was The Beings of the Light that came through with love and encouragement for me. Sometimes I would hear from my guardian angels, but more often than not it was The Beings of the Light. They told me they were present to help me discover and fulfill my soul purpose. As I asked them more questions, I received more answers, but not always in the manner that I was expecting.

Sometimes the answers came on the written page, sometimes they came in the form of thoughts that would appear in my head just at the right moment, and sometimes I received my answers through other people.

In our beginning interactions, The Beings of the Light did not tell me exactly where they were from, nor did I ask. I wasn't ready to hear the truth anyway. Like all loving and divine guidance, that information was revealed to me when I was ready to hear it without being tossed into rampant fear. They waited until the time was right. That time presented itself during the first weekend workshop I ever taught.

CHAPTER 2

Azez Revealed

"Make me a channel of your peace." – St. Francis of Assisi

Following the guidance of The Beings of the Light, I accepted a request to travel a couple hours from where I lived to teach my first spiritual workshop. I was nervous, but the Universe blessed me with a group of very spiritually advanced participants. I was still in the spiritual closet at this point in time, still holding a fear that people may shun me and tell me I was wrong for teaching this work. With such an advanced group, I didn't have to worry about sugar coating my material or worry that I would insult anyone's religious beliefs. The Universe put me in a very safe environment to start off my spiritual teaching career, something that has become one of my most favorite things to do.

When I was first preparing the workshop, I came to a place in my notes where I knew I wanted to insert an interactive exercise, but I didn't know what exercise to do. I was intuitively told that it would come to me, and to just leave it for now. I listened. In fact, I listened so well, that during the workshop when we came to the place where it was time to do the exercise, I still didn't know what I was going to do! I did what any good facilitator would do in the same situation. I bought myself some time by giving a fifteen-minute break.

The participants gathered in the kitchen and munched on their snacks completely oblivious to my inner panic. I went to the bathroom to be alone and think. I heard an inner voice say, "You can channel the next exercise."

"Did I hear that right? Did I just hear that I can channel the next exercise?" I asked in amazement. I have to admit, I was quite excited about the idea. Then my fear kicked in and said, "No way." The guiding voice in my head remained calm and adamant, "You can do it. You can channel the next exercise."

Intuitively, I knew it was true. I just wished I knew what I was going to say. Stunned, I came out of the bathroom and sat down in my chair. All the participants were still chatting and snacking in the nearby kitchen. I wanted to tell them to come and sit down, but I was unable to speak. The voice in my head whispered, "Be patient. They will come."

A moment later, the participants just stopped what they were doing, came back to the workshop space and sat down. I wanted to tell them that I was going to channel the next exercise, but again I was unable to speak my own thoughts. The light I was about to channel was already running through me. The next words I uttered were theirs.

Because I was working with such an advanced group, they all knew what channeling was and immediately recognized that I was going to channel a message. They perked up intently listening to what was going to be said. This is what they heard.

"Take a deep breath, close your eyes, and relax. Imagine that you have the ability to create stem cells. Imagine you are creating them right now. As you create these cells, notice how they begin to multiply, just as bubbles do when you place bubble bath in a jet tub. Allow the stem cells to multiply some more, until pretty soon you have thousands upon millions of stem cells at your disposal. Now, imagine that the stem cells are even brighter than you imagine them to be now. Make them sparkling light. Allow them to shine in their perfection.

These stem cells carry divine intelligence and know exactly where it is that they are needed most in your body. Allow the divine intelligence of these stem cells to make their way to where they are needed most now. Do not try to direct them. They know where to go. Allow them to attach to whatever part of the body is in most need of them.

Notice how the stem cells become part of you. Feel the new energy that these stem cells bring into your body. They carry your natural blueprint of perfection. Notice how they begin communicating with the existing cells in the same area, reminding those cells of their natural blueprint of perfection. As your cells naturally die off and reproduce, they will be able to reproduce with the new energy that is contained within the stem cells you have provided. In this way, we are actually changing the cellular memory of your existing cells. And so it is done.

Did you hear that, Dear Ones? It is done. We can hear your thoughts hoping that you did it right. We are telling you that you did. The moment you imagine something happening in meditation, it is indeed happening. The moment you doubt your creation, it is as if you undo what was just done. But do not worry, Dear Ones, for if you doubt yourself, all you need to do is go back and create again what is wanted. If you are persistent, eventually the creation will stick and manifest. The more you say, "Oh it didn't work." the more you undo and revert back to the original. Believe, Dear Ones, you have the ability to grow back and repair parts of you that you thought could not be repaired. The only reason why you haven't is that you haven't believed that you could. We are here to tell you that you can. You did. You have. Believe.

We are The Beings of the Light and forever in your service. Good-bye."

Finally, I was able to speak. I believe I said, "Wow." It wasn't only me who felt the power of the exercise. Each participant was experiencing her own version of wow. I knew that the reason I wasn't given the exercise prior to the moment it happened was because I would have talked myself out of channeling. I would have just relayed the message of the exercise or substituted it with something different. Either way, it would have been much less powerful than the way it manifested.

I was told this is why Spirit does not often give us a lot of advance warning of our manifestations. If we knew what was coming, we would talk ourselves out of it, or we would find a way to deny ourselves of it. I knew this was true. I guess this is also why patience is a virtue. It yields results that are far better than we can imagine for ourselves.

Another wonderful surprise that came out of the channeling experience was a confirmation of the wonderful beings I had already come to know in my automatic writing sessions. One of the participants had recently opened up to her intuitive powers. Often, she would spontaneously channel information. When The Beings of the Light identified themselves at the end of the channel and said good-bye, she immediately began nodding her head excitedly. She told me that The Beings of the Light were the same light beings that talked to her. She told me they were from the star Azez, and that they were here to help us remember our infinite potential and uncover our innate healing abilities.

I was so relieved that a second person recognized this energy. I knew it to be the most beautiful and loving of energies, but had never heard anyone else talk about them before. It was also The Beings of the Light's way to let me know they were a benevolent energy from a far away star. They did this in a very safe, supportive environment. I needed this. I had grown up being afraid of anything extra-terrestrial. I remember going to bed afraid after watching movies or TV shows where aliens would come to Earth and wreak havoc. My father was always interested in the idea of aliens and outer space. I remember as a little girl my dad saying that if a spaceship flew over the house, he'd be the first to jump onboard. I know now that he was just saying he would jump at the chance to go where no man has gone before. But, as a little girl, I was worried if aliens came, my dad would leave us forever. It scared me.

When I returned home from the workshop, I was having trouble accepting this new knowledge. Part of my childhood fear still remained within me. The Beings of the Light told me that extra-terrestrial meant "anything not of this Earth." When you think of it in those terms, then all souls are extra-terrestrial, for they do not come from the Earth, but from Source Energy, or God. We are ET by nature, because, in truth, we are not human beings. We are Light Beings having a human experience. Any entity that you think of, whether it be an angel or a goddess or an ascended master is extra-terrestrial, in other words "not of this Earth."

I realized I had always associated anything related to being extra-terrestrial as something to be feared. I thought that any energy that was ET had to be ominous, threatening, and wanting to overpower us. Nothing could be further from the truth. The Beings of the Light are definitely from the Light. They are the most loving, caring energy I have ever felt. They feel like home to me. They are not here to deceive or control us. They are here to assist us in owning our own divine power and help us to tap into our infinite healing potential. They want us to claim our ETness!

If this sounds alien to you, I don't blame you. It has taken me a lot of time to accept that I am indeed in divine communication with a ball of wisdom from a star called Azez. It sounds like science fiction or perhaps even the ramblings of a mental patient. For me, it has been the greatest blessing of my life. The Beings of the Light have provided me with the means to heal the hurts in my life and the knowledge of how to move forward in my life in a way that brings me joy. I am not asking you to believe me. I don't need you to. But if you are searching for answers, ways to heal your hurts, and the means in which to live your life in a greater state of joy, perhaps my story and their wisdom can help you. Perhaps introducing you to The Beings of the Light will bring you the feelings of love and support that they have brought me. This is my greatest wish for you – to find your way.

My first experience of publicly channeling The Beings of the Light provided me confirmation that I was not the only person who was aware of their existence. Since then, I have met others who receive divine guidance from The Beings of the Light on a regular basis. There is one person I know who is on a similar path to mine, who often receives the same healing techniques I get from The Beings of the Light, confirming for both of us that we are indeed receiving divine guidance from the same source.

The channeling experience also led me to know that The Beings of the Light were here to provide me innovative, powerful healing techniques to help both myself and others. I share these techniques with you throughout the course of this book by first describing my experience then giving you the steps of how to use them for yourself at the end of each chapter, where applicable, in a section called Applying the Wisdom.

Please know that you do not need to be aware of intuitive abilities or channel The Beings of the Light in order for these techniques to work for you. All that is required is the belief in the possibility that they can work for you. Just as The Beings of the Light described to us in their channel, the moment we doubt what we are doing, we undo our creation by now making a new creation of doubt. Believe and keep the faith. Miracles can happen for you. They have happened for me. But they cannot happen if you decide in one moment they can't. This is how powerful our thoughts are. They create our lives for us, moment by moment, through what we intend, through what we decide, and through what we believe.

Applying the Wisdom

1. The first step to using the stem cell healing technique described in this chapter, and any technique found in this book, is to believe it can be that simple and it can be that easy. The most powerful creations come from simplicity and ease. Most people think something this simple and easy can't work, thus making it so with that very thought. If you think it has to be hard, it will be. If you think it won't work, it won't.

2. Close your eyes and imagine that stem cells are appearing and multiplying just beside your head or somewhere near your body.

3. Brighten the stem cells using your imagination by making the cells shine with sparkly light.

4. Allow the stem cells to move into your body knowing that they know where they are most needed. Let them attach to your body and interact with your other cells.

5. It's done. Give thanks for the gift of the stem cells and feel gratitude for the blessings and healing you have received. It's important that you actually feel gratitude and not just say thanks whilst feeling cynical and doubtful. The latter will leave you with results that will justify your cynicism and doubt. The former will leave you with results that will justify your gratitude.

6. It may be useful to repeat this exercise every day for 21 days, not because it is necessary, but because the belief that it can happen may not be as strong as the belief that it cannot. The repetitive application of this exercise and the feeling of gratitude for it will help form a pattern of belief so that it can and will work for you.

CHAPTER 3

How I Came to Know Who I Am

"The two most important days of your life are the day you were born, and the day you find out why." – Mark Twain

In January of 2012, my family vacationed on the big island of Hawaii. One of the highlights of the trip was visiting Volcanoes National Park and hiking the Kilauea'Iki Crater.

The crater is enormous measuring approximately 40 stories down and 2 miles across. When we reached the middle of the crater, I found a spot to sit on my own while my family explored. I then performed a little ceremony by burning incense and leaving tobacco as an offering. I was asking the energy of this place, which felt like the seat of creation, to allow me to remember the healing wisdom of ancient Lemuria.

In spiritual circles, Hawaii is believed to be the resting place of Lemuria – an advanced, ancient civilization, much like Atlantis. Many say Lemuria is mythical, just as many say Atlantis is mythical. For someone like me, who has experienced many past life memories, Lemuria is as real to me as North America is. In any case, I had become very interested in utilizing Lemurian wisdom to increase my ability to serve others in a magical way in this life. During my meditation in the crater, I didn't receive any immediate big a-ha moments nor did I receive any knowledge of ancient healing secrets, but felt that I had received a download of energy that would enter my consciousness when the time was right.

I packed up my things and gave thanks for the information that was forthcoming. I had a strange impulse to give an offering of thanks by pouring water onto the ground. As I watched the water disappear into the cracks of the black lava rock, I was thinking, "I should be saving this water for drinking. I'm going to need it later." But I couldn't help myself. I poured almost my whole bottle of water onto the ground, leaving only a few swallows for myself. I capped my bottle, caught up with the rest of my family, and enjoyed the rest of the hike.

It wasn't until I returned home that the download of information I received in the crater began to present itself to me.

One night, while I lay in my bed in meditation, I was taken back to the spot in the crater where I asked to remember the wisdom of Lemuria. A new set of beings introduced themselves to me and identified themselves as The Beings of the Earth. They sprung from the crater's floor like boulders. They were enormous and looked very much like the face statues on Easter Island. Their energy was very warm and loving. I felt embraced by their presence. They were incredibly grateful to me.

I was confused as to why they would be grateful to me. When I asked, they said, "You brought us the water." I remembered pouring the water from my water bottle onto the ground. "Oh," I replied. "No problem."

They told me I did not understand what they were saying. They asked me if I knew why I had poured water onto the ground that day. All I knew was that I had to. It was as if I could not leave without pouring the water onto the ground. They replied, "You asked to remember. That was part of your remembering. When we said thank you for bringing us the water, we were not talking about that day, although we were very grateful for it. We were talking about when you brought the water to the Earth long, long ago, before the humans had come."

"Your origins are not from Earth. You have always known that. Your soul comes from the star Azez. You are one of The Beings of the Light – the ones you communicate with often. It was The Beings of the Light who brought water to the Earth and you are of them. You, and others like you, brought us the water and we are most grateful because it was you, and those like you, who brought the possibility of life to the Earth."

My head was reeling with this new information, yet I knew it was true in my heart. It just felt right. Just then, The Beings of the Light appeared to me and welcomed me home. They welcomed me for finally accepting who I was. They said they had not revealed my connection to them prior to this moment for two reasons: 1. I had never asked, and 2. I had spent my time as a human knowing I was different and wanting to fit in. I had essentially denied who I was in order to conform and blend in with the other humans. I had also felt I would be persecuted for being different. This I already knew. I just hadn't made the connection that the reason I was different was because I was not from Earth, but from a far away star. As crazy as it all sounds, I knew it was true. It was as if many mysteries were unlocking within me all at once. I was beginning to remember.

"I can't be the only one." I thought.

"You aren't. There are many of you."

"Why do I feel so alone? Why haven't I met any of them?" I said.

"They, too, have been shunned for being different. They, too, have denied who they are in order to conform. They, too, have been hiding. When you accept and voice who you are, you will find your friends. When you voice who you are, they will feel safe in admitting who they are. One thing is for certain, when you are a Being of the Light, even if you have forgotten, once you ask yourself the question, "Am I from Azez?" you remember. You immediately know the truth. So my Dear One, there is no denying who you are to yourself any longer."

And that was that. I still had some fear to work through, but it was easier somehow knowing why I was different. It was also comforting to know that I was not a misfit, but someone who came from somewhere, someone who belonged somewhere, and someone who was here on purpose.

As I began being more open and confident speaking about The Beings of the Light as a race of beings from the star Azez, others started coming out of the woodwork, just as The Beings of the Light had said. I began mentioning them, then channeling them, in all my workshops and the messages they provided resonated strongly with the participants. In a matter of a couple of weeks, I had met around ten people who felt their soul, too, was from the star Azez. This was miraculous to me. I was no longer alone in my weirdness. In fact, my weirdness was becoming more mainstream everyday. It seemed that my admitting my truth was allowing others to admit theirs.

The Beings of the Light told me, "Consider yourself an outcast and you will become one. Consider yourself normal and so shall you be. Consider yourself magical and miraculous, and watch the magic and miracles occur."

I have been noticing the magic and miracles ever since. You may think me to be crazy, but if this is crazy, I don't ever want to be sane again. I have never felt more assured of who I am and what I came here to do.

CHAPTER 4

The Healing Waters

"Water is soft; yet it has the power to move mountains." – Lao Tzu

I had washed away my fears of finding out the truth of who I was and had come to accept that my soul had indeed come from Azez. What I hadn't been able to piece together was the relevance of bringing the water to the Earth. I had many questions about this. If I did bring the water to the Earth, why did I have such a fiery nature? Why was I born under the fire sign of Leo? Why was my power animal a dragon – an animal that breathes fire? It didn't seem logical to have such a connection to fire when my soul came from a wisdom that was so closely connected to water.

I called on The Beings of the Light and asked, "Are you sure I didn't bring fire to the Earth instead?"

They laughed. "You brought water. We brought water. Your soul comes from Azez, a star whose energy is fed by the Central Golden Sun. The Central Golden Sun is not the sun that lights the Earth and your solar system. It is the Sun that lights the cosmos. It is the Sun that gave life to your sun and all suns in all the universes in all the cosmos. In essence, Azez is a fragment of the Central Golden Sun. In this way, we are very fiery in nature, too.

We carry the wisdom of water, but do not live in the water as a fish or a mermaid does. You must remember that water did not come to Earth in a 3-dimensional way. We did not drive trucks carrying tanks filled with water from Azez and dump the water onto the Earth. We did not create an elaborate aqueduct system or pipeline and flow the water from our star to your planet. That is not how it worked. Instead, we brought the wisdom of the water to the Earth. We brought a wisdom, and from that wisdom the water sprang forth. It manifested itself in physical form on the earthly plane. Water carries the wisdom of light consciousness. It knew how to manifest itself on Earth in the perfect way to provide life for this planet.

Because the wisdom of the water was carried to Earth from Azez, you could say that water is extra-terrestrial. Your scientists have long known the properties of water are unlike any other substance on Earth. When it freezes, water expands. All other substances on the Earth contract when frozen. When ice forms it floats. Most substances become heavier as they become denser. Water becomes lighter. Water is limitless in its being. Like Source Energy, it is infinite. You cannot destroy water. You cannot burn it and turn it to ash. Unlike other substances that combust when heated, water simply changes form and evaporates, but it remains a water molecule. Water is infinite, limitless, and travels from the Earth to the atmosphere and back, replenishing and neutralizing itself in the process. It cannot be destroyed or changed into something else. It is and always shall be water. Like your infinite self, water is eternal life. When a human dies, the water in the physical body slowly evaporates. Although it aids in the decay process, water does not decay and turn into Earth, as flesh and bone does. This is because water is not of the Earth. It is eternal, as you are. As you know, without water there would be no life on the planet. It is essentially the lifeblood of Gaia - Mother Earth - herself.

The wisdom that you brought to Earth is that of salt water - the water of your oceans and the water that courses through your veins. Blood is saline and it is no accident that it is. It is the natural

Earth process of evaporation that created the Earth's fresh water. The salt water that created the oceans evaporated and then rained down upon the Earth as fresh water. You are wondering how that is possible given the large amounts of fresh water all over the world. What you must understand is that when you first arrived on Earth, she was dense, hot, and windy. Evaporation occurred quickly and winds swept the rain clouds in various areas that eventually made the now existing lakes, rivers, and glaciers. Also, understand that when you first arrived on Earth, you were not human. You were etheric and, therefore, able to exist in the conditions of Earth at the time."

This was a lot of new information to absorb. There was still more to know. The Beings of the Light continued:

"It is of great benefit for you to understand the crystalline properties of water. Water is a crystal and works very much in the same way that clear quartz works. You can best observe the crystalline structure of water when it is at freezing point for that is when ice crystals form. Water exists in your world primarily as a liquid crystal, but just like clear quartz, it has a very stable structure and is highly programmable. It is this highly programmable property that we would like to address and make you aware."

I love crystals. Anyone who has spent any time learning about crystals knows the power and purity of clear quartz. The Beings of the Light told me very emphatically to view water just as I would clear quartz. For those who are not familiar, clear quartz has the following properties (as taken from The Crystal Bible, pg. 225 by Judy Hall):

Amplifies Energy

Absorbs, stores, releases, and regulates energy

Excellent for creating energy flow

Increases your auric field (makes aura larger)

Cleanses

Contains every color possible

Stores information like a natural computer

Aids concentration and unlocks memory

Is a master healing stone and can be used for any condition

Stimulates the immune system

From this list it is easy to recognize the similarities that clear quartz has to water. When we become dehydrated we lose energy and deplete our immune function. When hydrated we are energized, are better able to concentrate, and remember. When hydrated we will naturally have a healthy glow about us (increased auric field). Water obviously cleanses and creates flow. Water certainly contains every possible color; you can't make a rainbow without the rain! And water definitely absorbs, stores, releases, and regulates energy. Anyone who has used a hot water bottle can attest to that.

What The Beings of the Light wanted to bring to my attention is the ability of water to store information like a natural computer. Water, like clear quartz, is highly programmable. This is why clear quartz is a master healing stone that can be used for any condition. It can be programmed to do anything. The Beings of the Light want us to begin viewing water as we have been viewing clear quartz – like a master healing crystal.

The Beings of the Light continued to explain: "Water is a natural healer when drank in a pure or lovingly programmed state. The problem with much of the world's water today is that it has undergone intense negative programming. It has been programmed with people's fears. We offer you the choice to intend for the water to revert to its natural, original programming. Ask the water to remember that it is perfection, light, and love. In this way, you will immediately release the programming currently affecting the water and allow it to transform itself back to its original life-giving perfection."

I began doing this as soon as The Beings of the Light asked me. It was amazing how much better I felt in a matter of hours. Now, whenever I have a glass of water, I say to myself, "I am going to drink a glass of Liquid Love." That's my new term for water – Liquid Love. Whenever I use water, I intend for it to revert back to its original programming of love. I now bathe in Liquid Love. I wash my dishes in Liquid Love. I cook spaghetti in Liquid Love. As I continue to do this, I am amazed how much water is present in our daily lives. We use water to wash hands, floors, and clothes. We use water to plant, grow, and prepare food. We use water to flush toilets and water lawns. It's everywhere! I now have a new appreciation for water that I had been taking for granted. I began to tell the lakes, rivers, and oceans to revert back to their original programming of love. If many of us do this, collectively we can heal the water. It's amazing how quickly it can be done and it doesn't require protests or rallies or other forms of conflict to achieve. The only thing is we must do it everyday, even more than once a day. The Beings of the Light explain why:

"When you ask the water to revert to its original programming of perfection, it is done instantly. However, there is still a constant barrage of negative thought and action occurring in the world that still affects the water. Like a crystal in a negative space, it must be cleared often. Eventually, if the water can stay in its original programming long enough and for enough times, it will create a pattern of holding that loving programming. If you feel compelled, you can help the water daily in this simple way. The water will be grateful to you and in return you will feel the programming of your own water inside your body changing. You will feel yourself reverting back to your own original programming of love and perfection."

This is a simple exercise The Beings of the Light invite us to do every morning and/or evening: Take a deep breath and bring your awareness to the water inside your body. Notice that there is water inside your veins, in your organs, in your muscles and flesh. There is water in your skin, in your bones, and in your cartilage. Water is everywhere within you. Thank the water for being present and ask it to revert to its original programming of perfection. Notice any sensations you feel as this occurs. After a short while, you may wish to become aware of the water that runs within your home and property, city or town, and surrounding areas. Ask the water in these areas revert to its original programming. Enjoy what it is that you notice from this request. Do not try to help the water or control the process. Just allow the water to be what it wishes to be. You can't get it wrong. The water knows what to do. Enjoy the process. It is very easy. After that, allow yourself to become aware of all the water upon all the Earth, in all the bodies of all the humans and the plants and the animals. Become aware of the water in all the streams, rivers, lakes, and oceans. Become aware of all the water that is hidden beneath the surface of the Earth and ask it to revert to its original programming. Ask for its original wisdom to be restored and anchored. Remind the water that is indeed Liquid Love.

The Beings of the Light tell me that by doing this with a loving and open heart, it performs such a loving act of kindness that it will provide you blessings in ways that is unimaginable to your conscious mind.

For me, water has become very magical. I notice when I forget to drink enough of it in a day that I feel tired, dried up, and irritable. Replenishing my body with the Liquid Love acts like magic restoring my energy, good mood, and also increasing my intuitive abilities.

If you think you may be dehydrated, I encourage you to insert extra Liquid Love breaks into your day. In other words, drink more water. I will tell you from experience what to expect. First, you will find you have to use the washroom frequently. Please know this is a temporary inconvenience. Your body is using the much-needed water to flush away toxins it has been diligently storing away from your vital organs. After that process is complete, the body will relax and you will no longer feel the need to rush to the washroom as frequently. The pay off for going through this mild inconvenience is that you will feel more alert, lighter, and more energized. This is just one simple, easy, and effective way to improve your life.

Just as a side note, it doesn't work if you use coffee or soft drinks as your main means of hydration. You need the water to flush away the residue and toxins left behind from the coffee and soft drinks.

If you wish to dress up your water, fresh squeezed lemon or lime is a wonderful way to do so. You may also add therapeutic grade essential oils such as lemon, peppermint, or grapefruit to flavor the water. The oils will provide added benefit and not alter the cleansing effects of the water. Just be sure the oils you use are therapeutic grade. There are many oils on the market that are not meant for human consumption.

Water is life. If you are lacking in life, you are most likely lacking in water. Drink up, my friends. Program your water, drink up, and you will find your cup doth runneth over!

Applying the Wisdom

Begin referring to all water as Liquid Love. Feel gratitude for water as you notice its existence and the valuable part it plays in your daily life. Ask the water in your body and on Earth to revert to its original programming of perfection daily. Keep yourself hydrated. Do these things on a daily basis and notice how much better you feel.

CHAPTER 5

Crystal Clear Intentions

"Art is a personal gift that changes the recipient. The medium doesn't matter. The intent does." - Seth Goden

I wanted to learn more about The Beings of the Earth. I knew they were closely connected with The Beings of the Light, but that is all I knew. I called upon them in meditation and asked them who they were. They said that they were indeed friends with The Beings of the Light, but more specifically, are the entities who have made and continue to make all the crystals found in the Earth. They were unable to do this until the water arrived.

I asked why it was important for them to make crystals. I was told crystals are and have always been used to regulate the vibrational energy of the Earth. Because of the programmable nature of crystals, The Beings of the Light in conjunction with the High Galactic Council, two groups tasked with aiding humanity and Earth to evolve to a higher level of light and love, have been able to download information into the crystal caves that lie deep beneath the Earth's surface to help advance our existence and balance the energies as needed. The Beings of the Earth monitor and regulate this process.

They wanted me to know that there are many crystals used to regulate the Earth's vibrational frequency and advance our evolution. These crystals are buried deep within the Earth and remain perfectly safe from human tampering. The crystals that are mined for use and sale by humans do carry the same frequencies and are given as a gift to those who come to have them in their possession.

I asked about the crystal that was found in recent times named Azeztulite. What is its connection to the star Azez?

"Azeztulite is an extremely high vibrational stone that was brought forth to the Earth at this time to aid humans in their evolution to carry more love and light within their physical bodies. Those who use this stone will find that it requires the letting go of fear and lower energies that reside in their bodies. If the person who works with this crystal is resistant to the letting go process, there may be uncomfortable circumstances or conditions that arise for the person. This is why it is not advisable to handle this stone until one is spiritually, emotionally, and mentally ready. Azeztulite carries the wisdom of Azez and has been programmed by The Beings of the Light specifically to aid humanity in remembering their innate powers of divinity and multidimensionality."

Shortly after I met The Beings of the Earth, I was guided to purchase a piece of Azeztulite. The piece I attained is no bigger than the size of a penny, but it is quite literally the most powerful crystal I have ever encountered. When I hold it, it feels like a white spiral of light encompasses my body. Any resistance to this light becomes immediately noticeable. For me, I would feel tension in certain areas of my body, especially in the heart chakra. I had to learn to surrender to the power of this amazing crystal and allow myself to breathe with it instead of fight against it. When I did this, I could feel my inner fight, which included feelings of anger, hate, resentment, and fear, melt away. I believe it was working with the Azeztulite that allowed me to finally come to the place where I could write this book.

The beauty of Azeztulite is that it is a self-clearing stone. Unlike clear quartz, water, and most other crystals, Azeztulite will not absorb negativity or lower energies and never needs clearing or reprogramming. Instead, it transmutes lower energies by raising them up to a higher vibration. Azeztulite is a master stone that cannot be programmed to a lower level, but has the ability to upgrade the programming of other crystals including water.

The Beings of the Light say that the intent programmed into Azeztulite is so strong that no human or Earthly intent can alter its path. It contains a pure, solid, loving vibration and is meant to fall into the hands of those who will benefit from it and spread its message of empowerment and love.

I asked if they were upset about the crystal mining and the use of crystals by humans to wear as jewelry and decorate homes. They said, "Gaia (Mother Earth) gives nothing without permission. Nothing is taken from the Earth that cannot be replaced by Gaia if she so chooses. The crystals are for you to enjoy and to keep them in your hearts as a sacred gift. Crystals naturally carry a higher vibration and help you to advance your own evolution. Talk to your crystals and let them know your wishes, dreams, and desires. They will be happy to help. Just remember to keep your thoughts and intentions pure while working with crystals. They are highly programmable and if you program them with thoughts of lack, worry, or judgment, they will not be effective. Set your intent strongly for what you would like them to do, and avoid setting an intent that tells them what you do not want them to do. They cannot and will not interpret your intent. If you say, 'Keep away poverty.' understand that doesn't mean 'bring prosperity.' That is only an interpretation of what it means. If you mean, 'Bring prosperity,' be clear and intend it that way. The intent behind a statement of 'Keep away poverty' is one of fear. You are afraid that poverty will come knocking on your door and force its way into your existence. The vibration 'Keep away poverty' is similar to one saying,

"Someone's coming to take my prosperity away." Notice how this is not a powerful place of focus and the opposite of what is wanted. Keep your focus and your intent powerful, and you will have powerful results."

With that short message, The Beings of the Earth beautifully reiterated what I already knew, but perhaps was not always vigilant in following. Be clear with my intent. Stay focused on what I want. Avoid focusing on the unwanted. "So simple," I thought, "yet not necessarily so easy to do." To that I received a cheeky reply from them, "Then all you need to do is intend for it to be easy." I immediately understood, smiled, and thanked them for the easy, gentle lesson.

I spent the next bit of time going around talking to my crystals and really focusing with clear intentions of what I truly wanted. The crystals seemed to perk up their energy, as did I. It was quite amazing how much of an energetic buzz I was getting from the process. It never ceases to amaze me how beneficial it is to notice with appreciation the things you have around you and give them divine purpose. That's what I was told I was doing. Noticing and appreciating, then with clear intent giving my crystals divine purpose.

The Beings of the Light then appeared and gave me helpful suggestions of how to give divine purpose to other items in my house. I was impressed by their careful appreciation of all things, despite what judgments we may hold. Here are some of their suggestions:

1. With clear intent, ask your mirror to provide only reflections of beauty. (You cannot do this one with sarcasm. Use sincerity. Everyone has beauty and it is time we started intending to see it.)

2. Ask your food to nourish you in the most beneficial way no matter what it is that you are eating. The term junk food creates the strong belief that you are eating junk. Of course, it will not be beneficial to you. If you are going to eat food lower on the natural or nutritional scale, call it love food and

enjoy every morsel. It will do more for you than a forgotten piece of fruit or a vegetable that you say you hate. Begin noticing the intentions that you feed yourself by the way you address your food.

3. Thank your plants for being representations of the cycle of life and intend for them to clean the air.

4. Ask the pictures on your walls to radiate beauty and love, and represent the creativity and inspiration that it took to produce them.

5. Thank your furniture for providing comfort and function. Without them, you and everything else would be solely rested on the floor.

6. Every time you turn on a light, thank it for bringing more light into your life. Every time you turn off a light, thank it for allowing you to conserve energy and take a rest.

7. Every time you flush a toilet, thank it for flushing away the crap in your life.

8. Every time you turn on the TV, intend for it to joyously entertain you and send out vibrations of love.

9. Intend for your clothes to enhance your beauty and bring you comfort.

10. Thank the cat litter for absorbing foul odors and providing a warm, inviting place for your kitty to do her business.

As I read over their list, The Beings of the Light commented, "We noticed that you noticed our list included things that you do not normally appreciate. That is the point. You never realize how grateful you are for your toilet or kitty litter until there is none. They provide great function and value in your life. Give them appreciation and added divine purpose by serving as metaphors for safe havens to get rid of waste. You may laugh at the idea of the mirror reflecting only beauty, but if you allowed that, you would only see yourself as beautiful. We understand that you desire to eat healthful foods, but if you are not, should the food you are eating be punished with your ill thoughts? They only serve to punish you as well.

From our perspective there is only love. Love appears as light. When we notice dark, there is no judgment. We don't sit around and complain about the dark. We don't blame the dark for infringing on our light. We don't worry that the dark is going to consume our light. (They laugh). Dark can't consume light. Light consumes dark! When there is dark, we only see a place that our love can fill. That is the challenge that we present to you: when faced with something that feels dark, see it as a place that your love can fill. In this way, there is no need to fix or change what is there. It is in the loving, that the fixing and changing occurs. Either the situation will miraculously change on its own or you will be inspired to perform some action that will facilitate the change.

Let us provide you with two possible scenarios to illustrate our meaning.

Scenario A: You become angry that someone else hasn't cleaned the toilet and complain that you are the only one who can seem to notice the mess, while you scrub away.

Our interpretation: You notice the dark, are annoyed by the dark, complain about the dark, leaving a clean, unappreciated toilet, and a very dark, unappreciative you.

Scenario B: You realize the toilet needs cleaning, and you thank the toilet for letting you know it needs cleaning by producing an unsightly ring in the bowl and a foul odor. You scrub away the mess, feeling satisfied as you breathe in a new fresh scent.

Our interpretation: You notice the dark, are grateful for the light, gain inspiration and motivation to shine your light, leaving a clean, appreciated toilet and an appreciative, happy you.

The average person's interpretation of both: Same result. Clean toilet.

As you can see, it's not the same result. It's not about getting a clean toilet. It's about how much love you can feel in any given circumstance. When placed in a situation where you notice the dark, see it as an opportunity to fill it with your light. Do this, and you will find your happiness."

I was compelled to ask, "How does this help me to get my husband to clean the toilet?"

Answer: "We will give you two more scenarios:

Scenario A: You see the dirty toilet, complain your husband hasn't cleaned it, and complain to him that he never cleans the toilet. You clean the toilet. Your husband is annoyed by your judgment of him not being helpful, may or may not say some words of annoyance, and walks away.

Our Interpretation: You see the dark, tell your husband it's his fault that there's dark, and in a dark mood, you clean your toilet. Your husband sees your dark, matches your dark, and raises it with his dark words. He leaves in a dark mood.

Scenario B: You take time to notice all the things your husband does for you and your family. You feel the gratitude for his presence in your life. You tell your husband, with a sincere and grateful heart, thank you for all that he does. You notice the dirty toilet. You don't care that your husband didn't notice, because you noticed how much he does. You clean it with a grateful heart. This pattern may go on for awhile, until one day you notice that the toilet isn't dirty, because, for some strange reason, your husband cleaned it for you, giving you just one more reason to find love and appreciation for all that he does.

Our interpretation: You see the light in your husband. You tell your husband you see his light and thank him for it. He feels your light making him feel light as well. You clean the toilet from a place of light. As you carry on this light-filled intention, the light grows and manifests into what you want – to feel appreciated for all that you do.

Do you understand now that it really has nothing to do with who cleans the toilet? It has everything to do with how much light and love you carry in any given moment. Light begets light. Dark begets dark. You will never find light in a dark place until you turn on your own light switch. When you focus upon what your husband isn't doing, you have turned your switch into the off position. The moment you notice and appreciate what he is doing, you flip your switch into the on position. You are the only one who can turn that switch on and off, so stop expecting him to do it. He's got his own switch to look after, and you can't control it. But when you turn on your switch, it shows him how to turn on his."

I began to realize how much I expected my husband to flip my switch. No more. I could do it all on my own, better and faster than he or anyone else. I flipped my switch to the on position, and happily went to clean my toilet.

Applying the Wisdom

Become aware of your intentions and ensure they are focused on what you truly want instead of its opposite. Stating what you don't want is not stating what you do want. Be crystal clear with your intentions and you will have crystal clear results.

Notice the divine purpose in all the things you take for granted. Notice the value of the people and things around you. Notice the value you bring to the people and things around you. The definition of appreciate is to increase in value. When you take time to appreciate someone or something, you will feel your worth increase too.

When you notice yourself blaming another for your ill feelings or feeling emotions you would label as negative, flip your light switch into the on position by shifting your focus immediately on something you can appreciate or feel grateful for. In doing this, you add light to the situation and will experience a better feeling, more pleasurable result.

CHAPTER 6

Magical Multidimensional Metaphors

"When you change the way you look at things, the things you look at change." – Dr. Wayne Dyer

One of the most amazing lessons The Beings of the Light have taught me is how to use a combination of my intuition and imagination to identify and understand the true underlying cause of an issue and then change it to something beneficial.

Most people do not know how to access the subconscious mind. In truth, it is remarkably simple. You use your imagination. When you ask the mind to imagine what your issue looks like, feels like, sounds like, and in some cases smells or tastes like, you will receive a sensory description of the issue usually in the form of a metaphor. This metaphor is how the subconscious mind is interpreting the issue. When you use your imagination to change the metaphor, the subconscious mind then will sense or interpret the issue differently. You will have a different reaction or behavior, because the metaphor in the mind has been changed.

Let me give you an example.

Sally says, "I feel like the weight of the world is on my shoulders." This is her metaphor. Weight on the shoulders is always the taking on of responsibility that is not yours to take. Anything you are truly responsible for should feel like an honor and fun to take care of, not like an obligation or a heavy sentence. Imagine if you were actually carrying the world on your shoulders and you dropped it. All the people and the animals on Earth could get hurt. There would probably be a lot of anger directed your way. No wonder it feels overwhelming. No one should need to shoulder such responsibility. Yet, when Sally says, "I feel the weight of the world on my shoulders," her mind is interpreting it as if she is actually, literally carrying the weight of the world on her shoulders and thus responsible for everyone and everything in the whole world. Talk about making a mountain out of a molehill.

Now that the issue has been found, Sally can use her imagination to change her situation. She can carefully put the world down, place it back in its orbit, and let it and everything on it exist peacefully without needing to fix it. She could remove the feelings of responsibility by imagining everything that needs to be done being put in project files, and delegating those files like a project manager to angels to handle. She could also imagine handing some of the files to actual people she knows and say in her mind to them, "These are yours. You have asked me to take responsibility for you and your issues. I am not the best person for the job. You are. I believe you are ready to take responsibility for your own stuff. To help and guide you I have arranged for a band of angels to walk you through the process."

We do this process until Sally no longer feels like she is carrying the weight of the world on her shoulders and instead feels lighter and equipped to move forward. Because we have changed the picture in the mind, the mind has actually changed how it views the situation. Sally's mind no longer feels the weight of the world on her shoulders, because she put it down and delegated all the projects she was trying to handle back to their rightful owners. She freed herself and lightened her load. As a result, she feels free and lighter.

The Beings of the Light told me that this method is so incredibly effective because what most people don't realize is that the imagination is a gateway to the 5th dimension. In the 5th dimension, you can create instantaneously, which is why the effects of this method are immediate.

For those who are not familiar, let me explain the difference between the 3rd dimension, the dimension we see reality in, and the 5th dimension, the dimension where all is possible. The 3rd dimension encompasses 3 components (or dimensions): length, width, and height. In fact, when you have all these components present, you will visualize in 3D. The 3rd dimension is very fixed and to function in this dimension there are certain rules that apply. In this dimension, time is linear, moving from past to future. We can only be in one place at a time. We see things in straight lines and in polarity. On one end of the spectrum there is one extreme and on the other end is the other extreme. This is where we experience good and bad, right and wrong, black and white, and all that is in between. In the 3rd dimension, there is a beginning and an end point. We do use the term infinity in our math, but it is a difficult concept for the 3-dimensional mind to comprehend. We have an easier time believing infinity has no end, that it just keeps going, but have an extremely difficult time believing infinity has no beginning. In 3 dimensions, it is impossible to imagine that there is no beginning. You have to start somewhere.

In the 5th dimension, the boundaries of the 3rd dimension disappear. In the 5th dimension, there are two other dimensions working with the first three of length, width, and height. The other two dimensions are time and space. In the 5th dimension, you are not bound by time and space, but able to transcend them. Time is not linear meaning there is no past and no future. There is only now. In the time of now, there are multiple events occurring simultaneously. In the 5th dimension, every possibility exists. This dimension is infinite and, therefore, has no beginning and no end. It cannot be added to nor subtracted from. It is complete. In the 5th dimension, you can transcend not only time, but also space meaning you could be in multiple places simultaneously. This is how entities such as angels and The Beings of the Light are able to communicate with us. They are able to transcend time and space and, therefore, one angel could be assisting every human on the planet at the exact same moment. This is why we never have to worry about asking for assistance. We are not taking away help from anyone else who may have a more serious or pressing issue.

You may notice it is impossible to believe in entities such as The Beings of the Light with 3 dimensional thinking. The Beings of the Light describe the star Azez being some 380,000 light years away. In a 3-dimensional world, time is linear. In linear time, it would be impossible for me to receive a message from so far away. When I communicate with The Beings of the Light, I am accessing the 5th dimension, where time and space are not an issue. I can be with them and they with me in any moment.

When someone leaves Earth and passes on, their 3 dimensional body is left here for us to watch decompose, leaving us with the belief the person is dead. But since our spirit is not 3-dimensional, it does not die. It transcends time and space, and at the time of our death it re-enters the multidimensional world from which it came.

This became very apparent to me when my mother died in the fall of 2011. I missed her very much. I thought about her all the time. This bothered me and I began acquiring feelings of guilt, because I never thought about her very much when she was alive. I saw her perhaps a couple times a month and had a good relationship with her, but rarely did I spend much time thinking about her in between visits. In my grief, I posted on my facebook page, "Ever since my mom died I think about her way more than I ever did when she was alive, and wish it were the other way around." My wise spiritual friends sent back messages stating what now seems obvious to me: "That's because she's with you all the time now." and "You think of her more now, because she is with you more now." In 3 dimensions, I couldn't see that she was still here. In 5 dimensions, she's here all the time. Upon that realization, I let go of all the guilt I had been harboring, and whenever I think of my mother, I say hello and give her a virtual hug. It seems that the difference between suffering and peace is 2 dimensions.

Because we come from a multidimensional Source, we are multidimensional. We are a multidimensional being having a 3 dimensional experience. The next part of our evolution is to realize that we are a multidimensional being and to purposely and consciously access our multidimensional powers in our 3 dimensional world. By doing this, our finite 3D experiences become infinite or, in other words, they become 5D experiences. One way to achieve the 5D experience is to realize the power of our mind to create. This is where the imagination comes into play as a vital component to our evolution.

Our imagination is our gateway to the 5th dimension. In our mind we are not bound by time and space. We can go anywhere and do anything with our imagination. It is our creative tool. The Beings of the Light would like people to start using this tool more frequently. Their message is: "It is in the mind that the magic happens, but it is not magic. It is merely accessing a different dimension that does not play by the same rules as the 3rd dimension. There are no rules in the 5th dimension. Anything is possible. The only rules that exist in the 5th dimension are the ones you imagine as real. When you allow yourself to dissolve those rules and all the consequences you have created that go with them, you will be totally free."

The Beings of the Light have been teaching me to become aware of the many rules I have created and taught me how to break them with my mind. I have come to understand I cannot create what I cannot imagine. They have helped me to stretch the limits of possibility I have placed on everything. As I stretch those limits, the world opens up to me in the most miraculous of ways. Sometimes it feels like I am performing magic, but I have come to realize I am only creating what I can imagine. Everyday I imagine the possibility of more and more. This is how I grow. This is how we grow. When we come to the point when we can no longer imagine anything different we stop growing. Once something stops growing, it withers and dies. It is no wonder science tells us that when we keep the brain active through learning, it keeps us young.

There is no better time spent than with your imagination. When things don't feel good to you, ask yourself, "If I could describe what this is like, what would it be?" Your mind will instantly provide you with a metaphor. If it's an ax looming over your head, grab hold of the ax and grind it down to nothing so that it renders it useless. If it feels like a rope is around your neck, remove it and burn it. If it feels like something dark is lurking in a corner, turn on the light switch and see what it is. If it's a man holding a gun aimed right at you, turn the gun into a rubber chicken. If he still feels like a threat, dress him in a ballet tutu and put him in 5-inch stilettos. Have angels wrap him in a cloak of loving energy that tickles and watch him giggle like a little girl. It's your mind, your imagination. You can imagine whatever you want! Trust me, in this manner, dealing with your fears can be fun, not to mention incredibly empowering!

If you find you can't think of a way to change your metaphor, ask for angels to step in and show you how. Sometimes they will just appear and carry away whatever is bothering you. Sometimes they will show you the method that is best needed to bring forth the change. One time I was working with a friend who had an ache in her shoulder blade. She said it felt like it was ancient and was there for as long as she could remember. It was shown to me as a snake that had made its den in her shoulder blade and had no intentions of coming out. The snake represented the ancient energy. Reptilian energy is some of the oldest on Earth. I didn't want to imagine killing the snake. I never like to use the imagery of a fight or bringing harm, because I believe it only creates more conflict and harm for the person. Since I didn't know how else to get the snake out of her shoulder blade without causing a raucous, I asked the angels. Miraculously a snake charmer appeared playing a flute. The snake perked its head up, and slithered out of her shoulder blade following the charmer all the way to the horizon and into the Light. We filled the snake's den with loving, healing light so that no other critters would find their way in there. My friend immediately felt a release in her shoulder blade and the ache vanished. I didn't think of the snake charmer; the angels did. I was just open to being shown other, more beneficial possibilities, and allowed my imagination to bring them to me.

There are no rules to this game of magical multidimensional metaphors, but I will give you some guidelines that will produce faster, easier, and more preferred results.

Avoid using violence to change your metaphors. Any fight that you engage in creates conflict. When you engage in a war, even if you win, there is much damage on both sides. You always want to find a way to come out of your circumstances in a loving way. This is why I didn't kill the snake in my friend's shoulder blade. This would have only caused my friend more pain.

Love is the answer to every question. When in doubt, apply love. This is why angel imagery has such power. Angels are love and only work with the energy of love. Love and light are synonymous in the 5th dimensional world. Where there is light, there is love. Where there is fear, there is dark. You only need to light a match to dispel darkness. Shine your love and there is no demon strong enough to defeat you. Demons, or any dark energy, feed on fear. When in the presence of love, they dissolve and turn into proverbial puppy dogs.

We believe we need to kill or destroy our demons. The energies of needing to kill and destroy are based in fear and actually give power to the very thing we wish to defeat. Think of your nemesis as a neglected school child that is in desperate need of a hug. Ask the angels to come wrap their wings around this fear and give it all the love that it needs. It will disappear fast. Ask the angels to wrap their wings around you and give you all the love that you need, and see how you feel. You will have no choice but to melt your feelings of stubbornness, anger, and fear into feelings of love, forgiveness, and acceptance. If it doesn't, it is only because you are not allowing the change.

If you are blocking love from coming in, it is likely because you feel that you don't deserve the love being offered. Use your imagination to change this belief. If you believe you have been bad, ask yourself, "What if I wasn't? What if I was wrong about that?" Imagine all the instances that make you undeserving as appearing in a pile. Put that pile in the back of a golden pick up truck and have angels drive it away to the love dump. If you have skeletons in your closet, take them out and give them a proper burial. You could even say a few words in your mind, like a eulogy, to honor these skeletons and thank them for finally going to their proper resting place. One thing I have learned from The Beings of the Light is there is always a way out. Don't stop working with the imagery until you are free. You will find a way.

I worked with a client who had been sexually abused by 3 family members as a child. She felt trapped by them. She had done everything she could to forgive them, herself, and move on, but still remained trapped in her circumstances. I was given the imagery of her being surrounded by her abusers and was unable to get by, no matter what direction she went. I asked the angels what we should do. They immediately were by her side, lifted her up above the situation, and placed her on a path that was above where her old thoughts of her abusers lay. They literally allowed her to rise above her circumstances of the past and gave her a new path to walk on going forward.

If you feel trapped by your circumstances, find the metaphor of how you are trapped, then use your imagination to get out leaving you safe and free. If you find yourself in a dark room, turn on the light and find the door. If the door is locked, you will find the key in your pocket. If the door leads to another dead end, ask to be shown the escape route and follow what you are given. If no way is given, it is because you believe there is no way out. Tell yourself, there is always a way out and you want to know where it is now. All of a sudden the walls will fall away, or you will see an opening that you did not notice before. Ask the angels or The Beings of the Light to come light your way. They will. And you will find your way out.

Using this process, what you are actually doing is accessing the 5th dimension where anything is possible. If you can imagine it, you can create it. Your mind is already creating things through the metaphors it is giving you. Change the metaphors and you will change your mind. Change your mind and you change your experience. It really is an inside job.

What I love most about these magical multidimensional metaphors is that you no longer have to put forth effort into getting other people to change or act differently. When you change how you feel, hear, and view things on the inside, the outside world will change to match. It will seem like the people around you are changing, but the truth is, you are the one who has done the changing. You have changed your perspective, and therefore, your experience.

In metaphysics, the subconscious mind is represented by the element of water. Like the depths of the ocean, when you dive into the subconscious mind, you will find the hidden meanings as to why you do the things you do. Only when you dare to dive in, are you able to find the truth. It is the place where all the answers to your questions lie. It is the place where all the reasons why you think the way you think reside. It is the place from which all your creations stem. It is for these reasons that it is very beneficial for one to know how to navigate these depths.

The Beings of the Light are masters at navigating the subconscious mind. They have showed me how to overcome many obstacles of my own making and release trauma and heartache I have endured. I have come to realize it is in the subconscious mind where all healing occurs. When we heal the mind, all else is healed. No wonder water represents the subconscious. It is the place where all that is not wanted can be cleansed and washed away.

Applying the Wisdom

If you feel an ache or pain in your body, or have some issue that you are dealing with, describe it as a metaphor. Then use your imagination to change the imagery of that metaphor to something more beneficial or pleasurable. When you change the pictures in the 5th dimensional subconscious mind, you begin changing the experience in your 3rd dimensional reality. If you have successfully changed the picture in your mind, you will feel the difference and think differently about your issue. If the suffering remains the same, you have not let go nor allowed another possibility to take the place of your current reality. Keep working on it.

Here are some common metaphors and one of an infinite number of possible antidotes:

If it seems like:	Then:
An ax is looming over your head	Put on a helmet, grab the ax, and grind it down until it is rendered useless.
You are gagged or bound by a gag order	Take the gag out of your mouth, drink a glass of water, and speak. Burn the gag order.
You can't breathe	Imagine going into the open air and breathe in deeply.
You are drowning or can barely keep your head above water	Give yourself a life jacket, and have a rescue boat appear and take you to dry land.
Your hands are tied	Have the ropes turn to wet noodles and free yourself.
You are imprisoned or trapped	Turn the walls into paper and escape.
You are carrying baggage	Put it down and unpack.
You are stuck	Imagine what is holding your feet down soften and walk out of it.
A noose is around your neck	Take the noose off and burn it. Breathe.

You are putting your head on the chopping block	Turn the chopping block into a pillow or keep standing while sawing the block into tiny pieces.
There's a knife at your throat	Imagine the knife turning into a feather.
Someone's put a gun to your head	Imagine that the gun is a toy that shoots out a flag with the word BANG on it or have it turn into a feather duster.
You are going to drop the ball	Place the ball gently on the floor and allow others to help you.
You have too many things to juggle	Place all the items down in a line so that you can relax and get your bearings. Then, delegate tasks to a team of angels trusting they will get the job done.
You are walking on eggshells	Imagine you move around by levitating or sweep up the floor so that there's a clear path to walk on.
Everything is so loud that you can't think	Cut the power to the source of noise and sit in quiet. Breathe.
You have to hold everything together	Let go and let everything crumble to pieces. Relax as angels clear away the rubble and provide a place to build anew.

CHAPTER 7

Trusting My Intuition

"Logic will get you from A to B. Imagination will take you everywhere." – Albert Einstein

I feel it important to confess that I am not one of those spiritual teachers who grew up seeing things clairvoyantly or knowing I had a sixth sense from a young age. I didn't have some knowing of psychic ability that I shut down early in life. As far as I can remember, I was always in the dark about my intuitive abilities. It took me a long time to find my intuitive light switch and flip it into the on position.

The reason I tell you this is because there are many people who believe you have to be aware of your intuitive abilities at an early age in order for them to exist. Not true. I wasn't aware of mine until much later in life. Now, I own a thriving business giving people intuitive readings and assisting in their healing journeys. I teach workshops that show people how to recognize their intuition and to trust it. I channel information from The Beings of the Light that provides me with new methods of healing and ways to live my life more happily. Do not be concerned if you have never been aware of your intuitive abilities. They're there, in you, and in every single person. When you decide to discover them, you will. Just like most things spiritual, intuition requires trust, awareness, and faith in your ability.

Upon thoughtful reflection on this subject, I realized that I had actually been searching for my intuition from a young age. I remember always being fascinated by psychics and mystics. In middle school, I read all the books in the library having to do with the metaphysical. I read books on palmistry, astrology, and numerology. Even so, I was convinced I didn't have any natural skill or ability. In my late teens, I bought a pack of tarot cards. I never tried to interpret the messages intuitively, but read the meanings from the little guidebook that came with the cards. I assumed that I was not capable of intuitively extracting the messages of what the cards had to tell me.

I remember thinking how amazing it would be to be psychic. As I mentioned previously, I thought it would be the most amazing thing to channel a source of light. I envied anyone who could. I realize now that all this was my soul trying to let me know its purpose and passion. It seems my intuition was talking to me all the while. I just wasn't paying attention.

When I finally awakened to spirituality, I couldn't get enough of it. I would breathe, eat, and sleep spirituality. Still, I would endlessly ask the questions, "What's my passion? What's my purpose?" It was right in front of my face! I very much wanted to be an intuitive and spiritual teacher. What was holding me back was my own unwillingness to believe I could be. I have found this to be the same with most people.

I found my intuitive skills late in life, probably a year or two before I turned 40. Then I spent a couple of years learning to trust that the messages I was receiving were indeed intuitive and divinely sent. Even after I started receiving information from The Beings of the Light, I still didn't feel confident intuitively reading for other people.

I remember the day it finally hit home I could do this work. I would get together with two other women with whom I had taken workshops, and we would practice healing techniques on each other. One of the women in the group is extremely clairvoyant. She can see energy patterns, spirits, and pretty much anything in the non-physical world. What I began to notice is that the messages and imagery I was getting were the same as hers. We would describe the exact same things. This built confidence within me. It was validation that I knew what I was doing. Spirit knew I needed that validation and found a way to give it to me.

I doubted the messages and imagery I was getting because I actually don't see them. I always thought in order to be clairvoyant you had to see the images as if they were a real life picture or a movie. I learned that part of my intuition is knowing what I would be seeing if I could see it. I can describe imagery in detail, because I know what the imagery would look like if I could see it. I may not see a tall woman wearing a red scarf, but I know that there is a tall woman wearing a red scarf present. I just know. Understanding the truth about the varying degrees of clairvoyance helped me to understand that my intuition talks to me in a different way than others. This is the same with everyone. My intuition first talks to me through feelings. I notice first what something feels like. This is called clairsentience or clear feeling. I am then able to create a picture from the feeling. This is called clairvoyance or clear seeing. I am then able to have a conversation with the picture and hear messages. This is clairaudience or clear hearing. The truth is I feel it all and actually don't see or hear anything. I just know what I would see or hear if I was seeing or hearing it. This is claircognizance or clear knowing. For some people, they will even be able to ascertain messages from clear smelling and clear tasting. Take a moment to ask yourself how you intuitively gather information. Know that you never have to see a single thing to have access to intuitive information. Once you surrender to the idea that the messages you receive are indeed your intuition, and not your imagination, then you begin to open up to the wonderful world of magic.

When I finally gained the confidence to read people intuitively in my business, I realized that I was very accurate. Complete strangers would come to me and I could tell exactly what their thoughts and beliefs were. I intuitively found that I was able to tap into another's subconscious mind and read what is there. With the help and guidance of angels and The Beings of the Light, I then assist the client in changing the limiting beliefs within the subconscious for their highest good and the highest good of all involved. In this way, I am working on a person's mental and emotional health in a hands-off way.

Other practitioners access their healing abilities using hands-on methods such as Reiki, Quantum Touch, or massage. Some do readings where they relay messages to the person. Examples of these are psychics, angel readers, or mediums. Most people use their intuition to help them with whatever work that they do. You do not need to be in a spiritual profession to be intuitive or access your divine guidance. Doctors, nurses, plumbers, electricians, teachers, and people in every profession use their intuition to guide them to quick, easy solutions. Those that are not able to access quick, easy solutions are not accessing their intuition. They are, instead, accessing their ego.

As I stated previously, intuition comes in many forms. You just need to pay attention and trust the messages you receive. Understand that intuitive messages generally do not knock you over the head and drop a specifically worded note in your hand containing detailed instructions. They don't generally appear as an angel standing next to you telling you in detail and step-by-step what to do. While intuitive messages are sometimes that blatant and obvious, usually they are much more subtle.

I had felt compelled to write a book ever since I awakened to spirituality. I attempted to write one many times, only to abandon my attempts after a few short chapters. I was annoyed that Spirit was nudging me to write a book only to leave me high and dry once I started. Frustrated by this, I began asking why I wanted to write so badly but was unable to. Shortly after asking this question, I attended a seminar facilitated by Lee Carroll, a man who channels a group called Kryon. During the channel, Kryon talked about divine timing. They said you may know you want to do something, and therefore, assume you must do it now. Have you ever considered that perhaps it would be prudent to ask, "When should I do it? Is it now?"

Bingo! The big light went on for me. This was the answer to my question. I immediately asked, "Should I write a book now?" The answer was, "No." This prompted me to ask, "When should I write a book?" The answer was, "You'll know. If you don't know, then the answer is not yet." This put my mind to rest. I forgot about needing to write a book, until one day I woke up and just knew that it was time to start. I picked a day to begin, and never looked back. It was that easy.

I want to point out that when I asked myself the question, "Should I write a book now?" the answer I received was not from a voice I actually heard. It was more like I felt the answer. I felt that the answer was "No" and the guidance was "You'll know". I could feel the truth of them. I also knew when I asked the question, "Should I write a book now?" that the answer "Yes" didn't feel true. It felt like a lie. This is how intuition speaks or conveys its messages to me. I primarily feel the truth. Others just know or see or hear the truth.

When I realized that my ability to feel the truth was my intuition talking to me, a whole new world opened up for me. I realized that the reason I had not been aware of my intuitive abilities as a child was because no one around me understood the power of my ability to feel. When I would express my feelings to my family, they would tell me to not be so sensitive and to grow a thicker skin. They were telling me, through well meaning intentions, not to feel what I was feeling. Wanting to obey and be normal, I did my best to turn off my intuition. At the time, I didn't realize that my family was not feeling as deeply as I was. I thought everyone felt feelings in the same way. I reasoned that if they weren't letting these feelings bother them, then there must be something wrong with me. Subconsciously, I began covering up my feelings and then hiding them. I built walls of armor around me to try to protect myself from the feelings I was having. I became scared to admit my true feelings in fear that people would tell me I was wrong to have them. I became very well practiced in answering the question, "Are you ok?" with "I'm fine!" all the while smiling on the outside and not realizing that I wasn't fine at all on the inside. I, like so many others I have come to know, was ignoring my feelings of discontent until it finally came to a point in my life where I couldn't ignore my unhappiness any longer.

I couldn't understand what was wrong with me. By all accounts, I had the perfect life. I had a secure well-paying job, a loving husband, two healthy children, and a nice home in a good neighborhood. I had achieved more than I ever thought was possible, and here I was, feeling absolutely unfulfilled, lacking, and alone. My husband desperately wanted to help me, but he couldn't. My unhappiness had nothing to do with him, although I am sure I blamed it on him on occasion. I had to do this for myself. Lucky for me, this was right around the time I found spirituality. It saved me.

By studying spirituality, I learned what intuition was and the different ways it speaks through people. I discovered my intuition speaks to me through feeling. All my life my intuition was so acute, that I was actually feeling the feelings of others around me. As a child, I was feeling the stress of a father, a mother, three brothers, and two sisters on a daily basis, plus the feelings of anyone else I encountered at stores, school, and church, and thinking those feelings were my own. It is no wonder that I felt like such a mess. It is no wonder why I tried to harmonize any conflict and desperately wanted to fix people. If they would just start feeling better, then I could, because I was feeling their feelings!

The more clients I see and the more workshops I teach, I realize that the acuteness of my intuition is not a rare occurrence. There are many people, just like me, unaware of their intuitive abilities, feeling the feelings of others around them.

It can seem like a curse to feel other people's feelings, but the truth is, once you are aware of this power and you learn to manage it, it is an immense gift. This is how I read people. I tune into what they are feeling. From that, I can determine what thoughts and/or beliefs have created those feelings. Once I know the thoughts that create the feelings, it is just a matter of changing the thinking. Change the mind and you change the experience. My gift of feeling has allowed me not only to honor and understand my emotions, but also to be very effective at a job I absolutely love. It is the key to my receiving intuitive guidance. It also has helped me to be compassionate, something that is hard to be when you're busy trying to protect yourself while pretending to be happy all the time. I now know that I am not the only one who sometimes feels insecure, hurtful, jealous, selfish, victimized, or depressed. I now know it's ok to feel something other than "perfect". Through compassion, I have been able to forgive myself for many of my feelings, and accept that I am human, and therefore, allowed to make mistakes.

For those of you who become annoyed and disgusted by someone who tries too hard, or who tries to control everything, or who can't seem to get past their own selfish desires, or who won't let you in, or who can't allow themselves to be vulnerable, cut them some slack. They likely have had to shut themselves off from feelings that were too hurtful to face. Your love and compassion for these people will melt the harshness away and provide a safe haven for them to face the demons from which they are hiding. Your judgment only serves to create more of a hostile environment in which they will hole themselves deeper. I speak from personal experience. These people are not mean, selfish, stupid, or shallow, just as I wasn't. They are hurting. Unless you have felt this pain, you have no idea how much.

If you are a person who is highly influenced by the moods of others, feels compelled to fix other people's problems, or pretends everything is ok when it's not, you probably are someone who is able to feel other people's feelings. Understand that you can separate other's feelings from your own. The Beings of the Light have been instrumental in helping me to manage my empathic intuition. (An empath is someone who feels the feelings of others). An absolute must is surrounding yourself daily, and even sometimes more than once daily, with sparkly light. I always notice when I forget to do this. Without the light, which acts as a purifier of energies and emotions of others, I notice my mood and my energy level dropping. Even if you don't think you're an empath, this is a good practice to make a habit, because, in truth, we are all empathic. We pick up the energy of others whether we realize it or not. Do this one thing, and you will begin to feel better and have easier, happier days.

Surrounding oneself with light is done intuitively. You just imagine that it's happening. Remember that your imagination is the gateway to the 5th dimension, and when you imagine with belief something happening, it is. I like to surround myself with white sparkly light followed by a layer of golden light. When I surround myself, I encapsulate myself in an egg of light, so that no negative energy can find its way into my energy field from any angle.

The other trick to managing empathic intuition is when you begin feeling something unpleasant out of the blue, whether it be an emotion or a physical pain, ask "Is this mine?" If the answer is yes, wrap the feeling and yourself in love and light. If it's not, then ask your higher guidance to separate your feelings from the feelings this emotion or pain belongs to so that you no longer are uncomfortable. Then, ask that love and light be sent to the feeling and person who is feeling the emotion. Simple and effective. And yes, it is that easy. Trust and believe.

If you find that you are feeling the feelings of others, but are unable to separate from them, then you have decided to take responsibility for that person's feelings. Your ego likes to do this because this makes the ego feel important. What could be more important than being responsible for another person's emotional well-being? The truth is, you are not responsible for anyone's emotional well-being but your own. Detaching from other people's feelings will leave you feeling free and joyful. If there is someone you wish to help, empower them by staying in your own light. If they ask for help, assist them in letting go of their negative feelings. If they don't ask for help, allow them the freedom to feel their feelings, no matter how negative they may be. Taking their feelings on as your own does not free them from their emotions. It just creates a dependency rendering them powerless to manage their own emotions. This is similar to the notion that if you took on someone else's suffering or illness, you would render them well. You don't. It just makes two people ill instead of one. While your suffering may help others to not feel alone in their suffering, it does not release it. It just makes it that much harder to get out of it, because twice the suffering is now in each person's experience. Again, I cannot stress enough, manage your own well-being and you will empower and assist others to manage their own. Try to do it for them, and you will end up overwhelmed by the impossible responsibility you have taken on. In turn, they will end up always looking to you to make them happy, leaving you both in a place of powerlessness.

The reason I am able to feel other people's feelings is because we are not separate from each other. We are all One. When I work with a client, I feel their issue and ask them to feel it with me. As I let go of the issue, they let go. I can feel it happening. The more I allow the release, the more they allow it. In truth, I am not working on them, but on myself. If I don't have the issue in myself, then I will not have a client with that issue. As I help others heal, I heal myself, and vice-versa. We really are that interconnected. The most successful healers in the world do not work on the person's illness or issue. They work on releasing the piece of that issue that resides within them that makes them able to see the issue in another.

I can hear a number of objections to this way of thinking already. "I have a client who has cancer and I don't have cancer. It's not my issue." I used to think this too. The Beings of the Light have taught me how to recognize the truth that we are all One. Anything in my outer experience is a reflection of something that is going on in my inner experience. The outer world mirrors the inner world. I may not have cancer, but I may be holding onto a belief that cancer is almost impossible to heal. I may have an emotional hurt that is similar to the emotional hurt that caused the cancer to manifest within the client in the first place. I carry part of it within me. That is why it is in my experience in the form of a client with cancer. I am being given an opportunity to heal within me what is hurting within them, and vice-versa.

I admit I believe that cancer can exist. I am working on adopting the belief that cancer is easy and simple to eradicate from the body. This way, I become much more effective in my healing and ability to assist others in adopting this belief. If we, as a society, believed cancer was no big deal, it would be no big deal. We also need to realize that sometimes people will create a big deal in their lives for a reason. Sometimes what we view as negative is actually purposeful. Sometimes people are ready to leave their physical body and they subconsciously know this is an effective way to achieve that. Sometimes people want to overcome a challenge or dramatically change their perspective, and this will do it. None of this is done consciously, of course. No one consciously says, "I want to get cancer." But our thoughts and beliefs are always subconsciously at work creating scenarios for us to accept, learn from, rise above, or use as a means to an end.

I know that my belief that any person can change, has the power to leave their unwanted circumstances, and create wanted ones is part of the reason I am good at what I do. I believe in miracles. I believe in magic. I am successful in creating them everyday. Before I see a client, I always create a sacred circle around my office, invite in divine help from a number of realms, and purposely intend for magic to happen for the highest benefit of all involved. This is my intent for every session – to let the magic happen. It always does.

If you think that I am a Pollyanna that is off her rocker, then it is safe to say that you don't believe that we have the ability to create magic and miracles. It's not that you're wrong. It's just what you believe. What you believe, you will experience. I believe in magic and miracles. It's not that I'm right. It's just what I believe. What I believe, I experience. I experience magic and miracles everyday. This illustrates the importance of challenging our beliefs. If things aren't going well, perhaps it's time to ask if it has to be this way. What if it is just a matter of changing a belief? What if this isn't just how things are, but just what I believe how things are in the moment? Imagine how you might be able to change your world knowing you are only one belief away from what you want.

My intuition has led me to challenge many beliefs that I have had about myself and about society. It has led me to appreciate the diverse field of possibilities from which we can choose our beliefs. It has helped me to know that others do not need to believe what I believe in order for me to be ok. It has also shown me the way back to my true heart's desires and the path to who I truly am. I no longer wish to pretend to be something I'm not, or pretend to believe in something I don't. This is my wish for you and for every person on the planet – to find your intuition and allow it to lead you to your true self, whatever that is, dropping all the beliefs along the way that tell you you're wrong.

Applying the Wisdom

Ask yourself how you primarily receive your intuitive guidance. Do you primarily see, hear, feel, or know your answers? Here are some clues as to how to determine which is your primary source of intuition. (Know that we have all of these intuitive outlets. This is to determine your strongest source of receiving intuitive information.)

Clairvoyants – Think and see in pictures. On a vacation, you look for spots with beautiful scenery. You like visual art, appreciate beauty, and notice the appearance of others.

Clairsentients – You imagine how others will feel in certain situations. You like movies for the way they make you feel. You enjoy people for the way they make you feel. You may feel like you need to fix people or be closed off emotionally as a means to protect yourself from all the emotions you encounter on a daily basis.

Clairaudients – Hear messages or voices that speak to them. You are aware of the tonality of people's voices as a clue to what they are really saying and view situations by the way it sounds to you. You love music, tones, and anything that has to do with sound.

Claircognizants – Have a strong inner knowing that cannot be explained by logic. Claircognizants are sometimes viewed as know-it-alls. You like to analyze, strategize, and figure out the plot or mystery. You have a strong gut instinct.

Ask your intuition to show you what your life will be like one year from today. Without controlling or creating what you want the answer to be, allow whatever comes to mind to surface. This is your intuition talking to you. You may see images, hear messages, feel what is happening, and/or just know. Allow your intuition to communicate with you often by allowing its guidance to surface in your imagination. Remember, our imagination is a key component to receiving intuitive information and is a vehicle for delivering the magical multidimensional metaphors that exist in the subconscious mind.

CHAPTER 8

The Bully and The Boxing Ring

"The most important decision we make is whether we believe we live in a friendly or a hostile Universe." – Albert Einstein

I was bullied in elementary school. Kids would tease me everyday. They would tell me I was ugly. They would find any reason to be mean to me. This bullying really eroded my self-esteem and hurt me very deeply. As is the same with all those playing the role of victim, there was a part of me that believed that what the bullies said must be true, why else would they say those horrible things? There must be something wrong with me.

It was during this time that my mind began creating ways to protect myself from the pain of the judgments of others. One way was for me to ignore the bullies and disengage from the situation. The mocking would be going on right in front of me and I would just ignore it as if nothing was happening, pretending that their insults were not affecting me, even though they were. This way, I would not be showing the bullies that they had power over me. Disengagement from others was my first protection mechanism. As long as I cocooned myself in my own little world, no one could penetrate. I built thick walls around me during this time in my life.

My next mechanism of protection was to judge other people before they could judge me. This way I always had the upper hand if attacked. If I could find something wrong with them before they could find something wrong with me, then I had ammunition to use in case I needed it.

Finally, my mind protected me by allowing me to become self-absorbed. As long as I kept an eye on how things might affect me, then I could keep myself safe from future attacks. It seemed to me at the time that no one else was thinking of my needs; why should I be thinking about theirs?

Oddly enough, I made it through elementary school and by the time high school came, I was very adept at conforming to popular standards. I had lots of friends and was very social. My protection mechanism of disengagement made me a master at not allowing anyone to see what I was truly feeling. This made me pleasant to be around. I was always "fine". The mechanisms of judging others before they could judge me and of self-absorption seemed to be par for the course and very normal in high school. It appeared that I had not only survived, but was finding a way to fit in.

As I grew older, my protection strategies were no longer effective. They started working against me instead of for me. I realized I didn't want to be what I had become. I wanted to be more engaged with my husband and family. I wanted to be kinder, gentler, and less judgmental. I desperately wanted to interact with the world, even though I was terrified at how it might treat me.

After I discovered spirituality, I began to meditate for the first time. Through meditation, I explored the feelings that I had hid away from childhood. It was a painful but liberating process. Finally, I was facing what I wasn't able to face in middle school. I spent many nights crying myself to sleep as I let out all the tears that were valiantly stuffed away by a strong little girl many years ago. I came to the realization that I had acquired a great deal of anger, resentment, and shame from these past experiences. I knew in order to ever be truly free of it I had to forgive my past, forgive the bullies, and forgive myself. I tried, but I just couldn't.

Over the years, I had grown immensely spiritually. I had become a brighter, better person in many areas. This was my one nemesis. No matter how hard I tried, I was unable to think about my childhood and not feel the pain. Whenever I thought about the bullies, one in particular, I felt betrayed, hurt, and helpless. I didn't know how to let it go. This is when The Beings of the Light stepped in to help me.

They showed me that I was living life from a defensive perspective. Every time I walked into a new situation, I was on the defense. I would hang back and wait to see if it was safe for me to be there. It was like I was always on the lookout for henchmen, never free to say or do my own thing in fear of being attacked and persecuted. I may have been an adult, but I was still living in fear of being bullied. I spent my life walking on eggshells, and waiting for the ax to fall.

Life is viewed through a lens. The picture you see in front of you depends on where you point your camera. My camera was pointed at danger. I held a perspective that I lived in a dangerous world. What I needed was to change my perspective, look around and find a different picture to take with my camera. It was time to stop seeing the world from the view of the dark back alley and begin seeing it from the sunny neighborhood street where kids laugh and play and where love lives.

My mind couldn't even imagine that new perspective. Where I came from, the neighbor kids teased me, and I didn't have a clue where love lived. I asked The Beings of the Light to take me to a new perspective and show me.

As I closed my eyes, I felt myself being unscrewed from the place where I was standing, the place from which I viewed the world. Needing to be unscrewed demonstrated how fixed I was in my position. I had dug in my heels unwilling to budge. As The Beings of the Light unscrewed me from this place, layers fell away. The layers were the layers of protection I had built up to shut myself off from the cold and dangerous world I stuck myself in.

The next thing I noticed was that I was being placed in a boxing ring. I had my gloves on and was very frightened. Dark surrounded me. The Beings of the Light spoke softly to me.

They said, "Fay, turn on the lights and look around. What do you see?" I was expecting to see an angry crowd hurling slurs my way expecting me to fail and a big, mean opponent on a mission to get me. When I looked around, no one was there. I was alone. No one was there to mock me. No one was there to fight. "Where did everybody go?" I asked, but I already knew the answer. They were never there.

The Beings of the Light said, "You are always ready for a fight. That is why you never let your guard down. With your guard up, you can never let the love in and you can never let the love out."

"I'm protecting the love!" my subconscious shouted back.

"From who?" they asked.

"From the bullies."

"Where are the bullies?" they asked gently.

I kept trying to summon them forth, but they were nowhere to be found. This is when it sunk in. I wasn't in any danger. No one was out to get me. I was alone in the boxing ring. I was my own bully.

Shocked by this realization, I said, "All this time I thought I was protecting the love I had."

The Beings of the Light countered, "Love is the most powerful, strong, benevolent energy in the Universe. It doesn't need protecting. It's time to let your love out so that it can protect you. When you are surrounded by love, there is no danger."

At that moment, my heart went click. It was as if an imaginary force had taken a key and unlocked it. Light started to beam from my heart and grow so intensely that it surrounded me with a glowing golden light. I no longer was in the boxing ring but instead was transported to a beautiful place where everything looked kind, peaceful, and loving. Instead of judgment, I felt acceptance. Instead of fear, I felt the power to be myself without apology. It was as if I was given a new set of eyes.

"A new perspective is like looking through a new set of eyes. You are now seeing the Universe as it is, made of light. It is not the scary place you had imagined." said The Beings of the Light.

I imagined my childhood and pictured the bullies from my past. They seemed inconsequential. I saw how they used bullying as a protection mechanism to make themselves feel important. I saw how if I were to meet them again, I would not feel like I needed to hide myself or get them to love or accept me. It was no longer important, for I had all the love and acceptance I needed within me. I did not need to get it from outside sources any longer. I also saw how I could let go of my self-absorption and feel safe to open my heart to others like I always wanted. I was no longer lacking. I was enough. Finally, I was enough. In that moment, I knew this is what it meant to feel complete.

The Beings of the Light spoke again. "Whenever you feel yourself slipping into your old neighborhood with all the back alleys and boxing rings, open your heart and see through these eyes. These are the eyes of the heart. The eyes of the heart see only love, acceptance, and truth. They are the eyes of compassion and they forgive all."

Seeing through the eyes of the heart has been a journey for me. I tend to flip back and forth, but am becoming more comfortable relaxing into the perspective that this is indeed a friendly universe where I am safe and lovable. The more I allow myself to love and be honest about what I am truly feeling, the better the result. Whenever I try to revert to my old ways of self-protection, judgment, and disengagement, I find myself feeling scared and alone.

If you are one of those people who have been bullied or felt like a victim of other's harsh judgments, it is time to let down your guard, come out of hiding, and take the gloves off. Understand that you may be in a boxing ring, but there is no one there to fight but yourself. There is no fight except the one you have within. Be honest with yourself and admit the truth of what you are feeling. By accepting you are hurting, you find the compassion within yourself to love, forgive, and console that piece of you that you have beaten down for so long.

Applying the Wisdom

Part A

1. Close your eyes and allow yourself to become aware of what you are feeling. Are there any tensions in your body? Do you feel pain? Do you feel emotion? Allow your awareness of these things to surface without judgment or trying to change what is there. Hint: Pain and tension are always the fighting or attempts to block a negative emotion that is trying to get your attention. When you surrender to it, you allow the possibility of letting go.

2. Just allow yourself a moment to feel the emotion behind the tension or pain. Can you identify it? Is it fear, sadness, worry, hate, anger, insecurity, depression, jealousy, resentment? Allow yourself to pinpoint the core feeling. Note: Allow yourself to feel the emotion, but do not get lost in it. If you find yourself allowing the emotion to take you over, imagine yourself detaching from it, rising above your body and just observing what is going on. Observe yourself feeling the emotion, instead of experiencing yourself feeling the emotion.

3. Accept that this emotion is nothing more than a cry for love and acceptance. Imagine wrapping the emotion in love and light. Ask your angels or The Beings of the Light to help you if you need assistance. Allow yourself to also be wrapped in the light. Breathe as you accept that you are ok to have felt this feeling and that you no longer have to fight it or pretend it doesn't exist. It is free to dissipate now, cocooned in a ball of love and light.

Part B

Sitting quietly with your eyes closed, ask The Beings of the Light to help you see the world as a friendly place where love lives. Ask to see from the eyes of your heart. See where this leads you and allow yourself to go wherever your imagination takes you. You may not have the same experience as me, but if you, in earnest, ask to be shown the way to where love lives, you will be taken there. If you find yourself in a place that doesn't look like love, do not fear. It may just be a pit stop on the way that needs to be addressed. Ask what lesson or wisdom you need to gain from this place, then watch and listen. My pit stop was the dark boxing ring. I needed to go there before I would allow myself to go to the place where love lives.

CHAPTER 9

The Power of Desire

"The starting point of all achievement is desire. Weak desires bring weak results, just as a small amount of fire makes a small amount of heat." – Napoleon Hill

You may have heard the expression: where there is a will there is a way. The Beings of the Light say that where there is a desire, a way will be shown. They very much want us to get back in touch with our desires, for they lead us to all the answers. Desire is the key to creation.

Think back on your life recalling things you really wanted, really desired. Notice that when you desired them and kept asking questions on how to fulfill that desire, the wish came true. Notice how when you desired something, and then believed that it was out of reach, how you stopped yourself from asking how to get there, and the desire remained unfulfilled. The belief that your desire was out of reach stopped the possibility of obtaining what was wanted in its tracks because you stopped questioning how to get there. You just assumed you couldn't. Your desire to see it through stopped when the questions stopped. Desire is very closely linked with our ability to question, which is curiosity, and our ability to believe, which is trust.

Every month a small group of my friends, who are also spiritual practitioners, get together for what we call an Energy Spa Day. We work on each other as a group, clearing our energies, removing our blocks, and providing guidance where needed. Getting together as a group is always very powerful. Imagine having four or five energy healers working on you at once. This is what our Energy Spa Day is.

During one particular Energy Spa Day, we sat in meditation asking to receive messages from The Beings of the Light. I immediately started to channel them. We were all waiting for them to spew forth some amazing wisdom that would change our lives. Instead, they just remained silent. The silence was making me nervous. I asked them in my mind to say something. They replied out loud through me, "What would you like to know? For we cannot answer a question until it is first asked. What do you want to know?"

Taking the hint, we began to ask questions. One of the first questions came from my friend Elaine. She knew my soul came from Azez. She wondered where her soul originated. Her answer was, "From Source Energy."

The Beings of the Light showed me a big ball of light that I intuitively recognized as Source Energy or God. I could tell that God is essentially a big ball of conscious awareness that encompasses every possibility of whatever has been and ever will be. They then showed me how one little flame of this light had such a strong desire to explore, that it broke away from its Source. This was the moment Elaine's soul was formed. She came to be through her immense desire to explore the vastness of All That Is. It felt like a child leaving home, ready to go make her own mark in the world.

They then showed me that her soul was well-travelled having visited many aspects of All That Is. Azez was one of the many stops on her journey. While on this journey, she has explored many different perspectives and points of view, which has given her an open mind and a deep compassion for people from all walks of life. This description resonated strongly with Elaine. She said it described her perfectly. It did.

Coming to know how Elaine's soul came to be ignited a desire within each one of us. We each began to ask where our souls originated from. Another lady in our group named Tracy received her answer right away. She was told her soul had also originated from Source. She was what The Beings of the Light called an Igniter – a spark that lit the flame. Her soul was a little spark that sprung from Source Energy and carried the wisdom and desire to ignite and spark the light within others. This is very much tied to her life purpose and describes her essence. In her presence, it is almost impossible not to feel the light within.

I was shown something slightly different. I was shown how the star Azez was formed. Like the individual souls of my friends, Azez also sprung from Source Energy. The difference was it wasn't a small spark or flame that sprung from Source Energy to create Azez. It was a ball of fire, so big that it created a whole star. Our group consciousness had such a strong common desire to serve the expansion of the Universe, that it sprung from Source Energy to create a star that still burns today. What keeps the star burning are the continued desires within the consciousness of the star. That consciousness is what we know as The Beings of the Light.

With a desire to serve the evolution of humanity, different parts of our group consciousness sprung forth from the star and became souls. I am one of those parts. First, I had a desire to serve by delivering the wisdom of the water to Earth. Then, I had a desire to serve in other areas of the cosmos. Then, I had a desire to be human. My soul carries the wisdom of how to be multidimensional in a 3-dimensional world and how to access the subconscious mind as a portal to the 5th dimension. Part of my soul purpose is to show other humans what is possible by accessing our multidimensionality and how to utilize that infinite power. I was told that The Beings of the Light who are serving as humans on Earth right now are the way show-ers. We are here to show others the way back to the heart.

There are many other humans on the planet who are Beings of the Light. Each are here to show others the way, but in their own way. The desire is the same, but the way it manifests will be different for every person. Perhaps you are one of The Beings of the Light. Perhaps, your soul is from somewhere else, but you have spent time dipping your toes in the Azez waters, and therefore, carry its wisdom with you. If you have a strong desire to know, all you need to do is ask The Beings of the Light to show you where your soul came from. Allow the answer to come to you through your imagination. Trust the information you receive. If you do not understand the information you are getting, ask for it to be shown to you in a way you will be able to understand.

Elaine's initial question, which sprang forth from a desire to know where her soul originated, led our group to realize the formation of souls, like everything else in creation, originates from a single desire. It also taught us a very important lesson that day. If you want something, you have to ask for it.

If you aren't asking any questions about your life, you won't get any answers. Every question gets an answer. Ask and it is given. This is also why it is important to ask the questions that will move you in the direction of your desired outcome. If you ask a question like, "Why does this always happen to me?" The answer will tell you why this always happens to you, but will not tell you how to get to where you want to go, because you didn't ask that question. Some great questions are "If I knew what my next move was to get me to my goal, what would it be?" or "How can this be better than it already is?" or "I wonder what it would take for what I want to happen?" Allow the answers to come to you. Don't try to answer them from your mind. Your ego doesn't know the answer to your questions. Your soul, which is your connection to your Source, does.

Sometimes it requires patience when you ask a question, because the universal forces need time to set up the delivery of your answer. When you do receive an answer, act on it, because it is the answer to your prayers.

The Beings of the Light say, "Pay attention to what you are asking. This will give you a clue to what answers you will be getting. If you keep questioning your ability to know by constantly affirming, "I don't know why this is." Or "I don't know how to change this." Or

"I don't know what to do", you will keep yourself in the dark. A statement of "I don't know" is not a question, and therefore cannot give you the answers that will lead you to know. A statement of "I don't know" is not stated from a place of trust or belief that you do know; therefore, the only possible creation that can come from this statement is one that leaves you believing that you don't know.

When you hear yourself saying "I don't know" change it to a question that will give you the answer. "If I did know, I wonder what it would be?" Keep asking that question, and soon you will find the answer plops itself into your thoughts as if by magic. But it's not magic. It is the summoning of your desire through the asking of your questions that cannot be denied.

What questions are you asking yourself? Change "Why does this always happen to me?" to "Something wonderful is coming my way. I wonder what it is?" Change "How come I am always surrounded by idiots?" to "I appreciate the strengths and abilities of those around me. I wonder what they are?" Change "Why am I a geek magnet?" or "Why are all the people I date losers?" to "I wonder who my ideal mate is? I wonder when and how I will meet him/her? I know s/he's out there and it is only a matter of time." That time will be soon if you keep asking this question and believing the answer is forthcoming. The question, when asked with sincerity and curiosity, creates a desire to discover the answer. The desire must be fulfilled and the answer will present itself to you."

The Beings of the Light tell me that many people will sabotage their efforts by giving up hope too quickly. When you ask a question and you haven't noticed the answer, instead of saying "this doesn't work for me", which will create a result of the process seemingly not working for you, keep affirming that you know the answer is coming and will arrive at the perfect time. You cannot create what you don't believe you can create. You can't have what you don't believe you can have. The moment you ask for something, it is on its way. By remaining curious as to what it is or how it will arrive, you keep the desire and belief alive. The moment you doubt it's coming, a doubtful outcome is on its way. The moment you tell yourself it's not going to happen, it's not going to happen. Yet, the beauty of it all is, in the next moment, you can ask for what is wanted one more time, and you set in motion the object of your desire to find its way to you once again. Where there is a will, there is a way. Where there is a desire, a way will be shown.

If we truly knew the immense power of our unyielding desire, we would make it our sole focus. The Beings of the Light have shown me many points in my life where I thought I was lucky or just in the right place at the right time, but it was the power of my desire that made the outcome, not luck. They tell me that the reason I was in the right place at the right time was because I desired it to be that way. They have asked me to include some of these points in this book to serve as examples of how powerful our desire is when you truly believe or at least refuse to doubt. I hope you find these examples simple and effective in illustrating the power of our unyielding desire.

When I was eighteen, I joined the Naval Reserve. I did not join to serve my country, or go to war. The truth was I joined to travel, meet people, and above all, have fun. I spent 13 years in the Naval Reserve and I have to say my overall experience met my intentions. I travelled; I met people; and I had a great deal of fun. I know that there are many people who did not and do not have this experience in the military. The Beings of the Light tell me my experience of the military was different from others because my desires were different from theirs.

One of the first things I was asked to do when I joined the military was to pick a trade – a job that I would be trained to do within the Navy. I looked through the list of various trades and decided immediately there was only one trade I wanted – Naval Signalman. Naval Signalmen were responsible for ship communications. One of the things they needed to learn was morse code. For some odd reason, I always wanted to learn morse code. I decided right then and there, this was the trade for me. I was going to learn morse code. End of story. My desire was set in motion.

I handed in my entry to my supervisor who came back to me and said I needed to choose another trade. When I asked him why, he said it was because women were not allowed in what was called "hard-sea trades". The only sea-going trade open to women was Diesel Mechanic. "Yuck", I thought. My other choices were Administration Clerk or Finance Clerk. I was interested in none of these trades. I told my supervisor the only thing I wanted to be was a Naval Signalman. He laughed and told me to think about it. He would need my answer in the next few weeks.

Due to my naivety about the government and its rules, I wasn't phased by what my supervisor said. In my mind, it was absolutely ridiculous that I couldn't be a Naval Signalman for the mere fact that I was female. In my mind, I was going to be a Naval Signalman, and that was that. It never even occurred to me that the rule was a government regulation.

Three weeks later, my supervisor came up to me smiling in disbelief. He said that I got my wish. I was a Naval Signalman. Somewhere between the time I last spoke to him to that moment, the government changed its policy and opened all hard-sea trades to women. At the time, I never even realized how big of a deal this was. To me, it only made sense. In my mind, the government had just come to its senses. It wasn't until I began conversing with The Beings of the Light that they brought up this example as a means to show me how my headstrong desire and ability to believe in what I wanted, despite of what circumstances surrounded me, was a blessing. They say I was instrumental in changing government policy. I have a hard time believing that this just wasn't good timing and that the policy was going to change anyway. They tell me that the change in policy was going to come through, but that it was planned to come into effect at a later date. My strong desire energetically forced the decision to be made sooner.

The Beings of the Light explained that in my youth, my naivety, my willingness to believe only in the possibility despite what others said or believed, allowed me to transcend the rules that other people believed had to be followed. This made sense to me. I remember early in my military career, a friend sat me down and told me that I acted like the rules didn't apply to me. He was trying to tell me to conform so that others wouldn't look down upon me. I did not take his advice to heart. I knew what I wanted and I didn't see how that was anyone else's business. Besides, I did follow the rules. I was punctual. I saluted and called the officers "Sir". I did my job, and very well for that matter. I was a very competent Naval Signalman. The rules to which my friend was referring were the unwritten rules that you had to pay your dues in order to get the good jobs. Dues seemed to refer to two things: the amount of time spent in the forces, that somehow being there longer meant you were more entitled, and how much time you had spent at sea, serving onboard a ship.

It's true. I didn't pay these dues. I never let the amount of time I had in the forces be a measure for the jobs I was entitled to receive. I also didn't enjoy being at sea for long periods of time because serving onboard a ship was extremely structured and strict. Since structure and strictness never seemed like much fun to me, I avoided those jobs for ones that seemed more flexible and enjoyable. Since I'm a teacher at heart, I spent more time focused on working as an instructor for the Communications Fleet School. And that's exactly what I did. It's not that I never went to sea. There was an opportunity to sail upon a warship for 3 weeks going from Victoria to Vancouver, then up to Alaska and back. This was a pilot project where they were sending 30 females onboard an all male warship to see how and even if a co-ed crew would work. This seems almost laughable now, but at the time, it was a big deal. Women had never sailed onboard warships before in any capacity. I thought this sounded like a great deal of fun. I applied and was accepted. The majority of the females selected for the trip were officer cadets, those in training to become officers. I was the only Naval Signalman. I guess you could say I was the first female Naval Signalman to sail onboard a warship. This made me feel proud. I served my country and my gender well on that trip. I did an excellent job and learned a great deal. I also got to travel to places I had not been before, made some very good friends, and had a lot of fun, which had always been my prime directives (travel, friends, and fun).

There was a great deal of people upset that I was granted this posting, because they felt that I had not paid the proverbial dues. Some of it was jealousy – they wanted to go and were upset they were not chosen. Some of it was righteousness – a belief that I had not earned my way to such an auspicious posting. The truth was I wanted to go and applied. I didn't pick me. Someone far away in National Defence Headquarters chose my name. As far as I was concerned, I had nothing to do with it. The Beings of the Light say I had everything to do with it. I had a strong desire to be on this posting and a belief that I deserved to be there, and that was why I got it. This is how we create our lives, through our desires, beliefs, and the questions we ask.

I asked The Beings of the Light what questions I asked in the above examples. They said I had asked what was the easiest way for me to have fun and move ahead in my military career. When I look back on my time spent with the military that was true. I was always looking for the easiest, most fun experience in all that I did. No wonder this angered those around me who had decided that they needed to work hard and pay dues to get ahead. My way was certainly more fun. I also realize I wasn't impeding on their experience, nor was it unfair of me to not play by their rules. That was their choice.

If you find yourself feeling like life is unfair, change the rules by which you live. You can do a good job, be skilled and competent, and have fun at the same time. I didn't excel in the military by being a screw up. I was good at what I did, and I had fun too. Don't live your life by other people's rules. You will be trapped forever. The problem with most people is that they desire other people's approval more than they do their own happiness. Instead of desiring the approval of others, desire the approval of yourself to do and be what you want. Throughout my life, I have played on both sides of that fence. Desiring other people's approval leads to an unsatisfying and unfulfilled experience. Fulfilling your own desires, despite what others think, always leads to happiness and fulfillment. It's a choice. Choose wisely.

Pay attention to your own creations. Your life is your own creation. Certainly there are others in your experience that are helping you create what is in front of you, but be assured that any hardship you encounter is not someone else's doing. They wouldn't be able to affect your experience without your consent or your continued focus upon the unwanted. When you take ownership for your creation, no matter how bad it is in your eyes, you have the ability to change it. Desire the wanted; believe in its existence. Notice that you must let go of the pain in order to feel the pleasure of your desire. Go to that feeling of pleasure. Ask how you can create more feelings of pleasure. Ask how you can find more ways to bring joy into your life. Whenever you ask a question, the answer is summoned from your internal desire. Your desire acts like a magnet to the answer of the question. Feel the answer coming and understand it is that feeling that your desire is summoning forth.

The Beings of the Light showed me how I wanted to create a feeling of ease and fun during my military experience, and that it was my unyielding desire to do so that afforded me the many opportunities that presented themselves to me during my military career. If I had been afraid that those experiences wouldn't happen, they wouldn't have happened. If I had believed that things like dues and government policy were impossible for me to get past, I probably would have lasted 13 weeks in the military instead of 13 years. They also showed me that by staying curious, I was able to create experiences throughout my life beyond my wildest imagination.

A Desire for Love vs. A Desire for Justice

The Beings of the Light say there is more love on Earth right now than there has ever been in all of history. They say that most people don't believe this, but instead believe the Earth has never been more full of hate, greed, and violence. In truth, it is the awareness of the hate, greed, and violence that has created a strong desire for its opposite. This desire has created a world full of love, generosity, and kindness. Even so, many feel there is a greater movement toward the unwanted. This is because people tend to take the news as an accurate measure for what is going on in the world. It is not.

The news provides a skewed perspective of what is really happening in the world. The news primarily focuses upon negative events. It will let you know if crime has happened, but rarely reports good deeds. It will show you instances of people corruptly using money, but forgets to show the giving, generosity, and kindness of companies and individuals. It will report the murders, rapes, and other violent acts, but does not tend to report the acts of kindness that happen everyday. It's not that there aren't negative acts occurring. It's just that they are not happening in the high percentages that people tend to believe when they use the news as a barometer for what is truly going on in the world.

When people become upset by what they view on the news, they actually add to the negativity of the very thing they wish would change. The more they focus on the injustices in the world, the more injustices will become present in their experience. Anger or fear towards a situation does not and will never make it go away. Adding fear to fear creates more fear. Getting angry with someone because they acted out of anger creates more anger in the world. Killing someone because they killed someone adds more killing in the world. Hating someone for something you do not approve of adds more hate in the world. None of these provide a solution because none of these focus on what is truly wanted – love and peace.

The Beings of the Light showed me this is similar to the reasons why our justice system fails to rehabilitate. Let's use the example of murder. Someone murders someone and is arrested. The first thing that they are told is that they are guilty and need to be punished. The punishment in this case is jail. While in jail the punishment continues. They are told they are there because they are horrible. People tend to fear or hate people in jail. They will even go so far as to say they deserve to be treated horribly. Eventually, that person will get out of jail. That's when society thinks the person should be rehabilitated. We expect them to act kindly and lovingly to others now. I don't know about you, but it doesn't take a rocket scientist to know if you kick a dog when he's down, he ain't gonna come wagging his tail at you when he gets up. In order for that dog to trust again, he's going to have to be treated very kindly and gently.

Imagine you do something that someone else or a group of people decides is horrible and requires you to be punished. As they sentence you, can you imagine yourself wanting to go hug and thank them for showing you the light? Or, are you angry and feel battered and bruised emotionally? Imagine being thrown in jail, treated harshly, told you are nothing but scum, and that you deserve this treatment as payment for what you have done. Do you wish to thank those who have judged you and look to them as wise mentors? Or do you just want them to go away and die? Imagine you are released after enduring this for one year or more. Would you feel like you wanted to make a contribution to society? Or would you feel like you had nothing to offer? No matter what someone has done or not done, do you think anyone deserves not to feel understood, accepted, and loved?

Love heals. Love is the only thing that heals. I'm not saying we should break open the jails and let everyone run free. It wouldn't work. What I am saying is that love needs to be added to the mix. It is difficult for me to imagine what a person must have to live through to come to a place where they willingly want to hurt someone else. Imagine the pain inside that person. This requires love and compassion to heal. Hate will not solve it. We can lock it away, but it will not go away. Only love can make it disappear. Only light dispels the darkness.

This begs the question; do you have a deeper desire for love or for justice? Be careful what you ask for, because you'll get it.

In one of my workshops, I met a woman who told me she carried anger around with her and didn't know how to get rid of it. She was angry about the murder of a close friend. What made it worse was that the woman who murdered her friend was now out of jail, and sometimes she saw her. Every time this happened, it brought back the memory of her friend's death. She became upset, seething with anger, and blamed this woman for not allowing her to enjoy herself. It was coming to a point where it was ruining her life.

I asked her if her current strategy of unforgiveness and hatred toward the woman was the solution. I asked if it was allowing her to feel peace. She of course said it wasn't.

I asked her then to think of what would be the best possible outcome given the circumstances. She said she wanted the woman dead. I asked her if, in her heart, she wanted to be responsible for another person's death. Was she really so cold-hearted that she truly wished death for another? She admitted she did not. She said she just wanted her friend back.

This is usually the problem when someone is unable to forgive. They want to go back and change the past. It's not possible. It is essential to accept what's done is done. Even if the one who murdered her friend wanted to change her actions, she no longer could. She can only change her actions moving forward. I compassionately said to this lady, "Knowing that it is not possible to bring your friend back to life, what is the best solution moving forward? Would it not be that the woman who murdered your friend comes to a place where she doesn't harm another person? Wouldn't the best outcome be that she become a beneficial and contributing member of society?" She agreed. "Then the next time you see her, send her love. Send prayers that she be guided to find her way to kindness. Ask that whatever it was within her that caused her to act in anger be healed within her. Ask that whatever is within you that hates her be dissolved into compassion and forgiveness." The woman said she never thought of it like that, but could already feel a difference within her. She no longer had to be angry and hateful. By changing her mind, she shifted her desire for justice to a desire for love.

I don't ever watch the news anymore, because the fear it instills in me is more than I wish to bear. I do not feel I am uninformed. Anything I need to know I find out. Anything I desire to know, I can search for myself on the Internet. I am not putting blinders on. I am well aware there is much love that is needed in all areas of the world. Where my heart takes me, I help in the ways that I can. This is how I choose charities, the petitions I am willing to sign, and volunteer work. This is my way to contribute and be part of a solution. I will never contribute to something that my heart cannot support. In this way, I give back to the world in a way that makes me feel good. By doing so, I add love to the situation I am supporting. This adds more love into the world, and makes me feel good at the same time.

I am not saying to stop watching the news. However, I do recommend watching with a different set of eyes. When you see something unwanted, send love and compassion to both the victims and the perpetrators. If it's a natural disaster, send love and compassion, not pity and worry. Imagine blessings and love emerging from the wreckage. Sympathy doesn't heal. Sympathy is feeling the pain and discomfort and does nothing to help anyone, especially yourself. Compassion allows one to honor where a person is at and provides the means to lift them out of it. Dump sympathy for compassion. Dump worry for love.

Many people think that worrying is a form of love. They believe it shows they care. Any emotion that leaves you feeling less than good is not love. I don't know anyone who wants to be cared for by having someone they love worry about them. If you truly care, send love and the belief that all will be well. Imagine it all working out. In truth, worry is a form of control. If we'd only learn to release control and surrender our worries to the light, we truly would feel and experience much more peace in our lives.

You may wish to ask yourself, "Where in my life have I been adding hate, blame, anger, or worry?" Change your thoughts about those areas to ones of compassion and love. Notice the difference in your emotional state. When we finally stop pushing against what we don't want and begin to send love to it, either through thought or loving action, we shift our focus to what we do want. This shift is a shift in energy, which will change you and the world for the better.

The degree of disconnection from Source that has occurred on Earth has created a desire of equal degree to connect back to its Source. This is part of the spiritual awakening. There is a desire on the planet to come back to a place of love. There is a desire to remember that humans are multidimensional and that we are Light Beings having a human experience. The desire is strong. Where there is a strong desire, the way must be shown. I am being shown my way partly through others on the planet, partly through my spiritual practice, and partly through my communication with The Beings of the Light. You may be shown your way through different avenues. The good news is all roads lead to love. Even the ones that go through the dark parts of town will eventually get you there. Just trust that your journey through the dark is temporary. Love is synonymous with light. When you can find love for yourself during the dark spots, a new light appears to show you the way.

Applying the Wisdom

What are your desires? It is very empowering to ask. It is even more empowering to know. When you want something enough, and keep asking how it's going to come to be, it must. There will always be those trying to knock you down or tell you the reasons why you can't. Remember, desire is not fulfilled by the relentless pursuit of pushing against something unwanted, but instead fulfilled by the relentless pursuit of finding a way to get there and believing a way exists. Where there is a desire, a way will be shown. Keep your focus on the wanted outcome, stay curious as to how it will come to be, and enjoy the ride.

Do you have a stronger desire for justice or for love? When we desire justice notice how an injustice must be present. Justice may even the score, but it does not end the game. Shift your desire for justice to a desire for love. Love not only ends the game, but eliminates it altogether. In its place, a playground of equality and forgiveness is created from which all can benefit.

CHAPTER 10

Uprooted Expectations

"To free us from the expectations of others, to give us back to ourselves - there lies the great, singular power of self-respect." - Joan Didion

One of the most limiting holds that you will ever experience is the need to fulfill the expectations of others. The need to fulfill other's expectations is much like trying to hit your mark by aiming at someone else's target. You may occasionally hit their mark, but never your own.

The Beings of the Light are very interested in assisting us to break free of the expectations of others. When we are no longer bombarded by other's expectations, we finally are free to be ourselves. They say:

"Humans have created many expectations over the course of their existence. Another name for these expectations are "the rules you must live by". We are here to tell you there are no rules that are necessary for you to live by, except the ones of your own making. For most of you, no one ever told you that you could make up your own rules. Instead, you fell into the belief that those before you fell into – the belief that the rules are set in stone and must be followed. Part of this belief includes the assumption that veering from the rules will lead to unpleasant consequences such as judgment, ridicule, death, and eternal damnation. God did not send you to Earth to follow a list of pre-assigned rules. God granted you free will. Free will means free to do as your heart desires. It does not mean, do it this way or else."

For many, especially those advanced on their spiritual path, it is common for the physical body to carry within its cellular memory the past life trauma of a harsh death due to the breaking of the rules or not following the expectations of society. I have memory of being put to death for being who I am. I have done a great deal of past life clearing to rid myself of the fear of doing spiritual work and being open about the metaphysical world. To those who reside primarily in the 3rd dimension, working in the 5th dimension seems like one is performing magic or miracles. In previous times, such skill was viewed as witchery and threatened the authority of those institutions such as the church and state. Those who did not conform to society's expectations were told they were doing the work of the devil, tortured, and killed. Most old souls experienced this harsh treatment and still carry the memory of it deep within the subconscious mind. It is no wonder why we spend most of our lives wandering around waiting for someone to harshly judge us then attack. It is no wonder why many of us are afraid to come out of the spiritual closet.

My soul has a strong desire to speak its truth. Throughout my life, I felt a passion to speak in front of groups, but when I did, my body would noticeably shake. This was the cellular memory being activated in my body as it remembered times when I spoke publicly, was persecuted, and put to death for what I was saying.

Through the help of spiritual methods I was able to release the fearful cellular memory in my body with regards to speaking in public. I can now speak in front of groups without violently shaking. I still find it difficult sometimes to embrace my knowledge and express my wisdom openly. It's tough to be honest when you think everyone around you is going to think you're crazy or lying. This explains why I would begin writing a book only to stop after the first three chapters. I was holding myself captive by society's beliefs and expectations of what was appropriate for me to do, say, and be.

Through meditation, I found out in the lives after my persecutions, I made a decision to keep myself alive by keeping my mouth shut, obeying authority, and towing the party line. This worked well for awhile, but in this life, my soul has a stronger desire to speak its truth in freedom than it has to live. In other words, I have come to a point where I have decided that I would rather die than stifle my truth. There is no point in being here if I can't be me. I also have decided to live, leaving me no other alternative except to speak my truth without fear of persecution or death.

I tell you this because I know it is the same for many of you reading this book. The Beings of the Light taught me a method to get past my fear and release the paralyzing hold of societal expectations that I felt was placed upon me. This method can be used by anyone at any time. I encourage you to use this method that The Beings of the Light explain in detail below:

"Sit quietly with your eyes closed. Imagine you are in a garden where the expectations holding you back are buried. At your feet you will notice there is a rope or a vine. Pick up this rope or vine, and tug on it. As you do, notice how you begin to unearth what will appear to be boxes. Each box will be attached to the vine, much like floats are attached to a rope that you use to separate lanes in a swimming pool. Keep pulling on the vine until all the boxes have been uprooted. There may be only a few boxes or there may be hundreds of them. It doesn't matter. Keep pulling until you can pull no more. Keep pulling until you feel nothing is left planted in the garden.

If you come to a box that is too big, heavy, or deeply buried to unearth, then imagine a band of angels appearing with back hoes and other digging machines. Have them dig the box or boxes up for you. Leave no boxes planted in this garden. Uproot it all.

The boxes represent the rules or expectations of others to which you feel bound. The smaller boxes represent the expectations of a single person like a parent or teacher. The bigger and more deeply buried boxes represent the expectations of society. They will have much more of a hold on you. We use the imagery of a box, because from our perspective this is what the expectations of others do to you. They put you in a box. The phrase "think outside of the box" really means think differently than what has been thought before. It means to free yourself from the confines of what has traditionally been done or expected in the past.

If you feel uncomfortable digging up these expectations, understand that you can make your own rules. You can even keep some of the old rules that work well for you. The difference is, this time it is your choice. You get to make the rules, not society, not your parents, not anyone else but you. You decide.

As the last of the boxes are uprooted, it is time to dispose of them. There is no need to think outside of a box if the box doesn't exist in the first place. Gather all the boxes up in a pile. Angels will help. Then, ask that a divine cleansing fire be lit and watch the boxes burn. The ashes that remain will feed the soil in a beneficial way, thus allowing the fear-based expectations to transmute to light. After the fire has died down and all the boxes have been turned to the fertilizing ash, allow your garden to be seeded with possibilities. In this way, you are replacing the expectations with new growth. You may also plant seeds of freedom, acceptance, unconditional love, and your heart's desires. This is your garden. You plant what you want to sow. Plant what you want to reap. The difference now is that *you* have planted the garden. No one has come in and said you must plant broccoli in your garden when you don't even like broccoli. Even if they say, "Everyone likes broccoli." You are now free to say, "Everyone but me. I wish you a bountiful crop of broccoli in your garden. My garden is going to grow corn." Society may say, "We don't like corn." And you will be able to say, "Then don't plant corn in your garden."

This method has truly helped me to feel free of the fear of moving forward in the direction I want to go. I know my road is the road less travelled, and feeling safe to follow it is making all the difference. I feel happy when I'm on this road. I never truly felt happy on the main road. Instead, I felt obedient. I know that the less travelled road is not a road for everyone. The main roads suit some people very well and if it makes them happy, they should stay on the main roads. It has just come to a point in my life where I must go off the beaten path. Perhaps it's the same for you.

At heart, I am a spiritual teacher who channels a group of wisdom called The Beings of the Light. My soul sprung forth from this ball of star wisdom and wants to talk about it. In essence, I am channeling the wisdom of my soul. It has never felt so good to finally admit that this is who I am and what I came here to do. I'm no fool. I know this is so far from the mainstream that it may seem like I am lost. I assure you I am not. This is who I am. I can no longer hold back who I am in order to make the majority of society feel comfortable. I am not the norm, nor will I ever be. The difference is now I don't care who thinks this is weird or strange. I like that it's weird and strange! The more I accept myself for this weird, strange person that I am, the more I find others are willing to accept themselves for whatever flavor they have come to spice up this big, beautiful world with. Admit and flaunt your strangeness. I guarantee it is what you came here to do.

I have a friend who embraces and owns his inner weirdness and strangeness in the most endearing way. He is a man who loves hot dogs and bacon. If there were a pedestal for food, he would put hot dogs and bacon on it. If hot dogs and bacon were deities, he would worship them. This is how deep his love for these foods lie. His favorite holiday is Groundhog Day. He loves this day so much that every February 2nd he takes a personal day, and celebrates it as if it were a statutory holiday. He loves airplanes and all things to do with aviation, but has a fear of flying. These are just some of his quirks. It would be easy for people to say, "He's weird." But the fact is, he is so totally happy with who he is that it is impossible not to love him for it. In fact, it would be tragic if he lost this "weirdness", gave up his love for hot dogs and bacon, and started working on February 2nd. Not only would this make him unhappy, but all of us who know him unhappy, because whether he realizes it or not, by being who he is, he allows each one of us to be who we are. It is part of his gift.

It is not your strangeness that brings forth ridicule from others. What brings forth ridicule from others is your unwillingness to accept your strangeness. Once you accept who you are and value your strangeness, others will too. I noticed when I embraced who I was and my ability to empower others in emotional healing, my business started prospering, my workshops started filling, and my reputation started growing. Once I stepped out of the spiritual closet and said this is who I am, like it or lump it, people liked it. I no longer received the lumps. I had to stop waiting for others to believe I was ok. I needed to believe it. Once I did, there was no doubt in anyone else's mind. It just became obvious.

Embrace your inner weirdness and strangeness. It is what makes you unique. It is also what inevitably will make you happy. Uproot the expectations of others that are planted in your garden and plant your own weird, unique happiness in its place. Once it begins to grow, you will find it will shine so brightly that others won't be able to help but smile. Pretty soon they will come around asking you where they can get some too.

Applying the Wisdom

1. A. Make a list of what you would like to do or be and the list of why you can't do or be it. Then make a list of all the things you do because you think you must or should, but would rather not. The list of why you can't and the list of what you must and should do represent expectations that need uprooting for you to move past them.

    B. Sit quietly with your eyes closed and affirm that you wish to uproot all the expectations currently holding you back from what you want to do or be. Follow through the method described in this chapter by uprooting all the boxes in your garden, burning them, and then planting new seeds of possibility in their place.
    C. Feel the gratitude and give thanks for this newfound freedom.

2. What do you hide from other people because you think it's weird or you think others will think it's weird? What if it isn't weird? What if it is unique? If you feel shame for what you are hiding, admit and accept what you are ashamed of to yourself. When you can embrace whatever it is as part of your divine experience, then it will not have such a hold on you.

CHAPTER 11

✴

The Holy Trinity

"Beyond a certain point, the whole universe becomes a continuous process of initiation." - Robert Anton Wilson

After I had uprooted many of the expectations that had been holding me back, I asked The Beings of the Light to show me more of my true life's purpose. I knew I was on the right track starting my business and performing spiritual healing sessions. I also knew that there was more, and I was ready to find out what it was.

One night, as I lay in bed meditating, just as I do every night before I go to sleep, my awareness was taken high above me. I was told I was being taken through the higher chakras. As I moved through four separate chakras above the crown, I came to what appeared to me as the top of the cosmos. I sat on the leading edge of creation looking out upon empty space knowing it was the fertile ground of possibility. The Beings of the Light asked me to turn and face the light. As I did, I found myself facing an enormous, expansive ball of all-loving light. I was told that this light was indeed what is known as the Face of God.

As I looked into the Face of God, a spark of its light separated itself and became a torch. The torch was handed to me. I was told that this is the light of God that I carry within. It belonged to me. I understood that this light was there to guide me and when I shine this light, I am home. I remember thinking, "I got the best part of the light." It was so beautiful and so vibrant. It was so me! I knew that every person on the planet was also given a piece of this light, each the perfect light for them to carry.

My torch of light was placed into my heart and I began to glow. I was then directed to look at myself in a nearby mirror. I was asked to see myself as God sees me, as light. The reflection was one that I didn't recognize and recognized at the same time. I was being shown the essence of who I am. I realized that in truth I was indeed a Light Being having a human experience and not the other way around.

Next, The Beings of the Light asked me to step directly into the mirror into my reflection. As I moved forward and stepped into my reflection, the mirror became a light portal. I was transported to an ornate room on the other side.

In this room, there was a beautiful ruby red crystal that sat upon a pillow that lay upon a pedestal. It was guarded by an angel who welcomed me into the room. The Beings of the Light spoke to me saying, "This ruby belongs to you. It is your soul purpose. You may choose to claim it as your own now. Please understand that this is a choice for you to make on your own accord. You do not need to take it now, nor will anyone ever force it upon you. It is your choice to own your soul purpose. Your choice and your choice alone. We cannot make the choice for you."

I wanted it the moment I saw it. I reached out my hands and took the ruby red crystal into my palms. I felt the warmth of the ruby as it began to glow. I placed the ruby into my heart where it nestled its way down settling into my sacral chakra, just below the belly button. The Beings of the Light spoke again, "This is your soul purpose that sits in the seat of creation. We activate it within you now."

As they said these words, the crystal began spinning and opened, shining its light, much like you would imagine a lotus flower blossoming. The feeling was overwhelmingly beautiful. Just as I was getting lost in the moment, The Beings of the Light spoke again. "We are not finished. It is time to move on."

I was motioned towards a door that was another portal. I instinctively knew that it led to somewhere I wanted to be. I went through the door and found myself in another ornate room. This time there was a large emerald green crystal lying upon a pillow on a pedestal. The guardian angel that watched over this crystal welcomed me. The Beings of the Light spoke again, "This emerald also belongs to you. It represents your heart's desires. You are free to choose to claim it as your own now. Again, this is your choice and your choice alone."

I was enamored with this crystal. It looked so beautiful and fragile that I was almost afraid to touch it. I reached out and placed it in my hands. Tears came to my eyes as I realized this was the missing piece I had been asking for. I almost didn't feel deserving of such a priceless gift.

Reading my thoughts, The Beings of the Light assured me that I indeed was deserving of this crystal. They told me the reason it seemed priceless to me was because it contained the true desires of my heart. It would not seem priceless to another, because my heart's desires are unique to me and can fulfill no other. I was also told that this was not a reward or something that needed to be earned. It was part of my birthright. Every person deserves to discover and live out their heart's desires. Holding back will not help any other move forward, nor will it be taking away anything from another. There is a crystal for every person that contains one's own unique signature. It is up to each person to claim and own it. Those that do, help those who haven't to find their way and make their own choices. It is a beautiful thing.

Their words helped me to make my decision. I claimed my birthright and placed the emerald crystal into my heart where it nestled itself. The Beings of the Light spoke again, "This is your heart's desires realized. We activate it within you now." Just like the ruby before it, the emerald began spinning and opening, shooting light beams in every direction. It was akin to my heart opening. The light of my heart's desires met and danced with the light of my soul purpose and synchronized acting as one.

There was another door for me to go through. As I stepped across the threshold I was transported to another room. This one was slightly different from the other two I had previously visited. This room looked regal. Surely, it belonged to royalty. Fabric of deep red velvet decorated the room. Everything else was bejeweled and made of gold. On a golden pedestal lay a golden crown. I knew instantly that it belonged to me.

The Beings of the Light spoke, "This crown belongs to you. It represents the divine mind. It is your connection to your higher wisdom. When people take off the crown of the divine mind, they lose their connection to their Source of Light. When people give their crown away, they give up their divine right to think and believe for themselves. It is your right to think and believe in a way that supports your heart's desires and soul purpose. When you give away that right, or believe that you do not have the right, it is impossible to fulfill your heart's desires and soul purpose. The three of these must be present and working in conjunction with one another to be fully realized. So now, if you are ready to take on the responsibility of thinking for yourself in a way that supports your heart's desires and soul purpose, please claim what is rightfully yours. Again, this is your choice to make and your choice alone."

I realized it was time to claim my crown and be the ruler of my own light. I had lived under the shadow of other's ideas and expectations for too long. It was time to be the person I came here to be – me! This is what I had been asking for. I was very grateful to be shown how to receive it. I placed the crown upon my head. It looked heavy, but was surprisingly light. It fit me perfectly. I felt like Cinderella trying on the glass slipper. Except this time, there was no need for a Prince Charming to come save me. Everything I needed I had within me all wrapped in three small packages.

Once the crown was on my head, The Beings of the Light spoke. "This is the crown of the divine mind that connects you to the infinite pool of possibilities. We activate it now." Upon those words, from the crown shot golden light in all directions that began spinning and spiraling upward connecting me to the infinite Source of all Wisdom. The light also spiraled downward synchronizing with the energies of my heart's desires and soul purpose, and continued downward anchoring itself into the center of the Earth.

The Beings of the Light explained to me that the three gifts I had claimed, the soul purpose, the heart's desires, and the divine mind, represented the Holy Trinity. Traditionally, the Holy Trinity consists of the Father, Son, and Holy Spirit and is usually seen as something separate from us. The Beings of the Light said it was now time to view the Holy Trinity as it is in truth – as part of us, and residing within. The soul purpose is akin to the Father – the one that gave us life. Our soul represents our eternal life, the part of us that carries on throughout all of time. The heart's desires are representative of the Son. It is the offspring of the Eternal Soul. The heart's desires are nothing more than the soul's wishes to express its purpose. Those expressions are the offspring of the soul. The Holy Spirit is representative of the divine mind. The divine mind is connected to the Source of Infinite Possibility and Divine Love that is the Holy Spirit. Together, the three of them make up who we are. We are divine beings. We are creators that hold the power and wisdom of Source, of God. Every person is. That is why there is not only one way, one belief, or one road to follow. There are an infinite number, and each one of us is here to explore our own road, develop our own beliefs, and express ourselves in our own unique way. Conformity was never part of the plan.

As I was trying to process all this new information, I was informed I had the choice to go through one more door. "There's more?" I asked.

"There's always more." was the reply.

Proudly wearing my new crown, and glowing from the inside out, I boldly marched to the new door that appeared to me. I stepped through it and found myself on the leading edge of creation. I saw a golden matrix made of light strands, much like you might imagine a hologram. I was given the choice to jump into this new part of the matrix. By doing so, I would be entering into a new perspective, joining the matrix in a place that would give me a new viewpoint.

I jumped and immediately was embraced by this grid of light. The matrix connected to me, to everything, and beyond. I wasn't in the matrix; I was part of it. I was one with All That Is connected by a web of light.

This was my introduction to the 4th dimension – the dimension of time. By being connected in the matrix to All That Is, I was connected to every aspect of me, every experience I had ever encountered, and every experience I had yet to encounter. I was connected to everything that had been created, everything that had yet to be created, and everyone who had ever been created or has yet to be created. Because all these moments of time existed in the infiniteness of this grid, they were all present at the same time. This is why the only time is now. Now, somewhere in the matrix, all that ever was and will ever be can be found.

My divine mind was working overtime, but I truly was beginning to understand the concept of the 4th dimension. It was now. The only time is now. Wherever I put my awareness in the now, is what I will experience. When I put my awareness on a moment that happened in the past, I travel to that point in the matrix with my awareness. I am not really in the past. I am still in the now. The reason I am able to observe that moment from the past in the now is because it really is occurring in the now, just on another point in the matrix.

Don't get too frustrated if this isn't completely clear to you. The important point of this is to realize that now is the most important moment you will ever experience. If it is not a moment you are enjoying, change it. Just like The Beings of the Light stated in each of the three rooms, no one is choosing for you. It is always your choice.

The Beings of the Light say that claiming our right to decide is one of the most powerful acts that we can make. Decisions are turning points that set the forces of creation in motion. No one can give you your soul purpose or heart's desires. They are innate, but you must decide to own them. No one can think for you, unless you decide to allow them to think for you. Either way, a decision has been made. A decision of inaction or powerlessness is still a decision. The good news is no decision is permanent. Another can always replace the one before, setting the forces of creation into a new direction. If you don't like what you have decided to create, decide something else. Indecision keeps people in limbo and doubt, always wondering which way to go. Just go! If you don't like where it's taking you, make a different decision and go in another direction.

For example, if you are in an unfulfilling relationship, you have three decisions available to you. Actually, you have an infinite number of decisions available to you, but this is just to illustrate the point. You can decide to do nothing, wait for the other person to change to make you happy, and wait in misery for a lifetime. You can decide to fulfill the relationship by reminding yourself what you love about the other person, appreciating them for who they are, and at the same time, remind yourself what is loveable about you and appreciate you for who you are. Or you can decide to leave the relationship to free you both to find someone more compatible. You could even decide what to do together, but if the other person decides a course of action different from you, you will need to decide whether to go along with their choice or follow your own.

The argument of "I don't want to hurt anyone." is one that people often use in this situation to delay their decision making. Making someone else responsible for your happiness is hurting not only them by placing impossible burdens on their shoulders, but also you as you keep yourself in a holding pattern of suffering. Making yourself responsible for another's happiness does the same thing.

In any case, always choose what feels best. I can guarantee waiting around for someone else to change to make you happy does not feel like the best option. It may feel like the safest option, but there is no happiness in your safe misery. Which decision makes you feel best? Choose that one and go, even if it scares you.

The Beings of the Light invite you to choose to re-enact in your mind my experience of receiving the Holy Trinity. They say that this is an initiation process where one comes to the choice to live one's own life from one's own power. I guide all participants that attend my

Spirituality for Beginners workshop through this initiation process. It never ceases to amaze me how powerful an exercise it is for people to decide to choose for themselves their own purpose, heart's desires and way of thinking. No one leaves unchanged. You do not need to participate in one of my workshops to receive this initiation. You only need to decide to do it for yourself. Follow along in the book, make your choices, and allow The Beings of the Light to do the rest. Enjoy claiming who you truly are. I know I have. I wouldn't have been able to write this book if I hadn't made the choices I did in the three rooms of the Holy Trinity. You may just be one decision away from something truly amazing.

Applying the Wisdom

Here is an abbreviated description of the Holy Trinity Initiation Process for you to follow for yourself.

1. Sit quietly with your eyes closed and ask The Beings of the Light to guide you through the initiation process.

2. Look into the Face of God and receive your spark of its light.

3. Look into the mirror and see yourself as God does, as light.

4. Step into the mirror and into the first room. Make the choice to claim the ruby crystal that represents your soul purpose and place it into your heart. It will nestle into your belly. Allow The Beings of the Light to activate it.

5. Step into the next room. Make the choice to claim the emerald green crystal that represents your heart's desires and place it into your heart. Allow The Beings of the Light to activate it.

6. Step into the third room made for royalty. Make the choice to claim the crown that represents the divine mind. Place it on your head. Allow The Beings of the Light to activate it.

7. Step out into the leading edge of creation and notice the matrix of All That Is. Jump into the matrix understanding you are now claiming the ability to see from a different viewpoint – from the view of the 4th dimension.

8. Come back to the present moment knowing that you have now embraced the Holy Trinity within.

CHAPTER 12

Freeing the Beasts Within

"You can't start the next chapter of your life if you keep rereading the last one." – Unknown

When I first started on my spiritual journey, it became obvious to everyone around me that I had trouble letting go. Spiritual healers and energy workers that had become friends and colleagues became very frustrated with me, because my will to hang on was very strong. However, their frustration was not even an inkling of the frustration I was feeling inside.

I made it my quest to figure out how to let go. I figured, if nothing else, I would do so out of sheer will. Little did I know at the time that my hanging on would serve to be a great gift. By figuring out how to let go, I learned a great deal about why I was hanging on. It is this knowledge that has made me a more powerful and compassionate healer. I understood my stubbornness and the reasons for it. I realized that no one hangs onto something without a good reason.

In almost every instance, the reason the subconscious mind will not let go is to protect you. The only reason you would need protection is because you feel you are vulnerable to or actually under attack. The subconscious mind views the act of protecting itself as a very real and necessary behavior. Like a pill, although some benefit is given, sometimes the protecting behavior will leave undesirable side effects. When the side effects become more problematic than the benefit, one feels compelled to make a change. In order to truly make that change, the subconscious mind will need convincing and to be shown another way to fill the benefit its current strategy is providing.

It may be useful to give you some examples of how the mind uses non-beneficial behaviors to protect itself. For example, a woman who cannot let a man into her heart may be protecting herself from rejection and a broken heart. She may even go as far as cheating or becoming verbally abusive in order to push him away if he gets threateningly too close. A man who gets angry for any criticism he hears may be protecting himself from feeling like he's a failure or that he is not enough. By telling the criticizer how wrong they are and becoming angry, the man allows himself to believe he is right and therefore, ok. A toddler who lies about breaking a dish is protecting herself from letting her parents know she makes mistakes and that she is not perfect. She may also be protecting herself from punishment. No matter who you are, at the very core of all this protection is a need to be loved. We protect ourselves so that we do not feel the worst feeling in the world – the belief that we are unlovable.

The Beings of the Light have given me a very effective and powerful tool to assist in letting go. While this method can be used for any scenario that requires letting go, I am going to use one of my clients who was unknowingly dealing with the after effects of childhood sexual abuse as an example.

I have not been a victim of sexual abuse; however, I have worked with many people who have been. I wanted to use this example because I believe the incidence of sexual abuse is far higher than we believe. I also want to show how the trauma of such a horrific experience can be much easier to let go of than we have been led to believe.

As is often the case, even when a victim of sexual abuse thinks they have dealt with the issue, often there are lingering non-beneficial effects in the subconscious mind that show up affecting relationships, career, and the ability to move forward confidently and fearlessly. Through the help and guidance of The Beings of the Light, I have been able to assist my clients to finally let go of the childhood trauma and move forward in their lives in a way they were never able to before.

Let's call my client Anna. Anna was unable to truly allow closeness in relationships. She kept her guard up when it came to men. She viewed men as authority figures that were not to be trusted. It is no wonder why she felt this way. It was two authority figures in her life, her father and an uncle, that sexually abused her as a child. To make matters worse, when she told a woman she trusted about what was happening to her, she wouldn't believe her. At the time, her subconscious mind could see no way out except to suffer in silence, so it devised a plan to keep an arm's length from any man or authority figure who may show interest. The mind also surmised that the best protection was for Anna to keep her problems to herself, because no one would help or believe her anyway.

It becomes pretty obvious that these protective strategies would become debilitating in her adult life. They served her well as a child, but were now causing far too many non-beneficial side effects. Something had to give. What was interesting is that she came to see me to help move her forward in her career. As far as she was concerned, she had dealt with the childhood abuse previously through counseling.

During her session, I was able to determine it was a childhood trauma that was causing the issue. This is when she admitted the abuse to me. At first I asked her if she was willing to forgive her abusers for what they had done to her. She said yes. Much of this forgiveness had already been accomplished from her previous counseling sessions. Then, I asked her if she was willing to forgive herself for having it had happened. It was obvious she was still harboring blame towards herself for the abuse. In her mind, she was still wondering how she could have stopped it from happening.

First, I had her accept the fact that at the time there was nothing she could have done to stop this from happening. If she could have, she would have. Often people are unable to forgive themselves because they think that they should have been able to make things different. They spend their energies on "If only I could have…" creating a ring of blame from which they cannot free themselves. Acceptance is the first key to forgiveness. I had Anna accept that what happened was done and could not have been done differently. She realized that in this moment she could not change the past, but she absolutely could change how she felt about it by moving forward.

The Beings of the Light had me have Anna imagine herself as the young girl who was the same age she was when she was being abused. I then asked her to imagine communicating with this young girl and ask her what it is that she needed. The young girl's answer was love. I asked Anna if she would be able to love this girl. She nodded. I then asked her to give this girl a hug and to provide her with all the love she could give. As Anna gave her young self the love that she was missing when she was a child, she began healing some of the pain from the past. But we were far from done.

I kept having Anna ask if the young girl needed anything else. We worked through giving the young girl understanding, compassion, safety, and freedom to be a beautiful, happy child. We also allowed her to confidently talk to her abusers and tell them everything that she wanted to say to them, but was unable to when she was young. I asked the angels to provide "young Anna" with anything else that she needed from the light in order for her to see herself as they saw her – perfect and innocent. The angels handed her a beautiful ball of light that they placed into her heart to have and to hold with her always.

Then, it was time for Anna to let go of the reasons she formulated in her mind as to why this happened to her. I asked "young Anna" why she thought she was abused. She answered because she was too pretty and because she had to obey those in authority. She also thought it must be because she was unlovable, why else would she be treated the way she was?

I asked The Beings of the Light to show me why this really happened to her. The answer I received even surprised me. First, I was shown that sexual abuse ran far back into the family lineage. Her father and uncle were doing to her what had been done to them.

I could feel their shame, pain, and confusion. Then I was shown that her soul agreed to come into this life knowing full well that she would likely be sexually abused. This surprised me. Why would a soul agree to such a thing? I was shown that Anna's soul agreed to endure the sexual abuse in order to put a stop to it once and for all. She came to stop the karmic pattern that had been running in her family for generations. Her soul cared so much that she was willing to go through this trauma in order to put an end to it forever. Imagine how much love and strength you would have to carry to agree to such a thing.

As I relayed this information to Anna, its truth resonated deeply within her. She knew it was true, because she vowed never to do this to anyone or let this happen to any of her children. The Beings of the Light told me that there were many other souls who have come to Earth for the same reason – to put an end to the pattern of family sexual abuse. They told me how these souls are strong and have a capacity to love much greater than the average person. They always decide to stop the pattern.

This knowledge allowed Anna to see herself in a brand new light. She no longer was a helpless child, victimized, and powerless to others. She was now a strong, loving soul with a purpose to put an end to the pattern of sexual abuse and heal her family's lineage at the same time. I can think of no greater act of selfless love. Nor could she.

Because the sexual abuse was a long-standing pattern that repeated far back into her lineage, also known as ancestral karma, I wanted to make sure the pattern was truly eradicated from Anna's lineage. I called upon Archangel Michael and Archangel Raziel to do this work. These Archangels are amazing at clearing karma and you can call upon them for help at any time. Archangel Michael is a master at cutting through fear and blame. Archangel Raziel is a master at clearing karmic patterns and past life trauma. I asked that Anna's entire lineage be cleared of any trauma, memory, karma, or patterns of sexual abuse in all dimensions of time, in all lifetimes, and for all eternity. This method clears the pattern not only for the client, but 7 generations back and 6 generations forward, including all siblings, aunts, uncles, cousins, nieces, and nephews. Indeed, Anna's soul had found a way to stop the cycle of abuse from reoccurring.

When I watch this process, it looks like light shooting in every direction clearing everything and everyone in its path. If anyone in the lineage seems reluctant to let go, I let them know that they will be freeing not only themselves from the pain and suffering, but also freeing the past and future generations from the pain and suffering. This is usually enough for those hanging on to let go and allow the entire pattern to clear.

After we cleared away the karma, Anna was brighter and happier, but her subconscious mind was still hanging onto the beliefs that it needed to protect itself from any possible future abuse. There was still a small part of her holding vigil, just in case she was ever put in a compromising situation. She was still seeing herself as a possible victim. It was time to let this go.

The Beings of the Light guided me in helping her let go of the fear of being abused again. This method works so well that I now use it in all instances in assisting my clients in letting go. Here it is:

I asked Anna to imagine all the worry and fear of being a victim of abuse and her abusers as wild dogs on the end of leashes that she held in her hands. I told her the reason she didn't want to let go of the leashes is because as long as she had hold of them, she felt she could control the dogs and keep an eye on them, and because she was afraid if she did let go, the dogs would attack her. Holding onto the leashes was her way of protecting herself. The truth was, the dogs didn't actually want to hurt her. The reason they were wild is because they wanted their freedom. If she let go of the leashes, the dogs would run away to the light and never return. I asked her to feel the leashes she held in her hands. I asked her to notice there was a band of angels surrounding her to protect her during this process. All she needed to do was let go - let go of the leashes and watch the dogs run away. I asked her to imagine just opening her hands and letting go. She did. She cried, as I made sure she watched the dogs run all the way into the distance until they became so small that they disappeared.

Afterward, Anna felt free and relieved. She had finally let go of all the trauma and lingering effects of her sexual abuse. I tell this story because abuse is not something that you need to suffer with for years. It can be released in the matter of an hour using these methods. I have witnessed it time and time again. The Beings of the Light say, "It is time to break the belief that suffering takes a long time to release. It truly can be over in a moment, if only you would allow the possibility. Ask yourself 'What if I were free?' When you have a strong enough desire to release something and the belief it can be done, even if you have no idea how, it will be done. You will be shown a way."

I have used the techniques described above to let go of many limiting beliefs and the painful memories of being bullied from my childhood. I imagined my bullies as the dogs at the end of the leashes and allowed them to run away. This may sound like an easy task, but can be difficult because it requires that you demand something different for yourself. It requires you take responsibility for what you feel and stop blaming it on someone else. It really is a choice to let go. No one can make your fear and pain go away but you. Once you make that choice, you'll wonder why you took so long, but do not lament on the time you wasted. Just be grateful you found a way and enjoy life moving forward.

Applying the Wisdom
Inner Child Healing

Anytime you have an issue, it likely stems from a belief you formulated as a child. It is beneficial to check in with your inner child often, ensuring it has everything it needs.

To connect with your inner child, imagine yourself as a young person, usually somewhere between the ages of 3-6 years old. Use your imagination to connect with this person. Tell them that you are them from the future and are there to help and love them. Ask them what it is that they need and listen for the response. Do not try to figure out what it is that they need. They will tell you. If you don't hear the response, you may feel it, see it, or just know.

If you are able, give your inner child everything that it needs. Hold nothing back. You cannot spoil your inner child. Your inner child does not need to earn reward or love. Your inner child deserves love unconditionally, just as you do, just as any small child does. If she wants a doll, give her a doll. If he wants a truck, give him a truck. Give hugs, pats on the back, or piggyback rides. Sometimes the child will want to play. Create a playground and let the child play. Sometimes the child wants a lollipop or candy. Hand it over with love. Don't tell her that it's bad for her and hand her a piece of broccoli instead. You want to be able to satisfy all the wants and needs of the inner child so that she feels complete, instead of denied. In this way, you feel satisfied. You will feel like you have received all that you need.

If you feel unable to give your inner child something that it is asking for, ask the angels to provide it for you. They will. Normally, they give their gifts as a ball of light or some other symbol of light that they will ask the child to allow into their heart and make part of them.

Keeping your inner child happy is a key to keeping your adult-self happy. When you really think about it, who are we but children who are just a little older? With this technique, you are never too old to have a happy childhood.

Letting Go Technique

If you are holding onto pain, suffering, guilt, blame, resentment or any other negative or non-beneficial feeling, use this technique.

Imagine whatever it is you are hanging onto, whether it is a feeling, a person, or thing, as wild dogs on the ends of leashes that you are hanging onto. Sometimes there may be only one leash and one dog and sometimes there may be several, even hundreds. It doesn't matter. It only matters that you are aware that you are hanging onto them.

Notice angels by your side so that you feel totally protected during this process.

Understand the reason you are hanging on to the leashes is so that you can control what is on the end of them to protect yourself, but the truth is you don't need protection from the dogs. The wild dogs only wish to be free and when you free them by letting go of the leashes, you also free yourself from the negative effects they bring you.

Now, become aware of the leashes in your hands and let them go. Open your hands and allow the pain and suffering (wild dogs) to run away. Watch them go straight into the distance and make sure they disappear. If they stay around or do not leave, it's not because they don't want to leave. It's because you haven't let them go. When you do, they will leave.

A Note to Those Who Have Experienced Sexual Abuse

Perhaps your soul is one of the souls that has agreed to endure the sexual abuse to put an end to the karmic pattern. If this resonates with you, it is. Congratulate yourself for your inner strength and deep capacity to love. Then allow yourself to let go of the pain, shame, and residual trauma by following the steps outlined in this chapter. Be gentle and compassionate with yourself as you go through this process. Sometimes it takes more than one try to let go. If you don't fully let go on your first try, don't give up. Keep working on it and ask your higher guidance for help. Eventually, you will find your way. Keep providing your inner child with all the love and support it needs as you go through this process. This is key to you feeling safe.

If your soul has endured sexual abuse and has kept the cycle repeating, understand that you can decide to change that at any moment. You can stop it right now, but you must forgive yourself first. Use the inner child and letting go practices outlined in this chapter to help you. Ask your higher guidance for assistance. Never give up. You can free yourself from this trauma. When there is a desire, a way will be shown. Keep asking to be shown the way out.

CHAPTER 13

✳

The Master Healer's Attunement

"Among all medicines there are none with the healing powers of love." – Masaru Emoto

Shortly after I began writing this book, I began feeling uneasy and uncomfortable, but was in the dark as to the reason. Something was bothering me, but I didn't know what. No matter what I tried, I couldn't seem to jump out of this feeling of angst. I hadn't been able to meditate or really feel connected to my intuition. When the feeling wouldn't go away, I decided that it was time to sit down and just commit to connecting and finding the answer to this problem.

As I began to breathe and empty my mind, I was forced to face the truth. I allowed myself to feel the fear and anxiety instead of trying to hide from it. I had learned long ago, that trying to hide from my feelings, or worse, cover them up by pretending all is well, did not work. The next question was, "Why was I feeling anxious? What was I afraid of?"

As soon as I asked the question, I received my answer. An uncle who lived far away had recently been diagnosed with prostate cancer that had spread into his bones. I had thought I was handling the news well, but to my surprise I was far more upset about it than I imagined I would be. As I sat honestly thinking about him, I realized I really loved him. He had spent a lot of time at our house when I was little, and I had grown very attached to him as a little girl. Now he lived far away and I rarely saw him. Little did I know, those childhood attachments still remained. I was feeling the fear of losing my uncle whose love I held deep in my heart.

I was relieved to find the source of my discontent. Now, I had power to do something about it. The solution seemed obvious to me. I was in the spiritual healing business; I would simply send him healing energy and then I would feel better.

I began to send him healing energy but I could tell he was blocking it. This frustrated me. I spoke directly to God, "There has to be something that can be done. Show me what it is!" I may have been frustrated and in tears, but I meant business.

The Beings of the Light immediately appeared and told me to sit quietly. I could feel a very intense, loving energy come over me. It was as if a column of golden light was showering upon me, but it was not a gentle shower. It was more like standing under Niagara Falls.

The Beings of the Light told me to relax and just allow the light to enter my body through the top of my head and exit out my feet allowing it to go deep into the ground. As I relaxed, the energy flowed smoother and it felt amazing. Just then, I noticed Jesus, the Master Healer, had come up behind me. He placed his hands on my head and shoulders. He was glowing the same golden light and I could tell he was transmitting ancient symbols into my body that carried knowledge of how to heal in the 5th dimension. He telepathically let me know that I would now carry these symbols with me, and whenever I needed to draw upon their wisdom to mentally or out loud say, "Symbols on." He told me that I need not know what the symbols were as I might find them distracting. I was to trust that the symbols would work in the highest and most beneficial of ways.

Next, I was asked to imagine myself in the Sea of Well-being. It was much like being in the waterfall of light except larger – the waterfall had turned into a sea! In this place, all was well. I was well. All was well with me and with everything. It was an incredible feeling.

The Beings of the Light asked me to imagine my uncle standing close by and to ask him to join me in the Sea of Well-being. I was about to go get him when they stopped me. They said, "You never have to leave the Sea of Well-being. You may simply invite who you want to join you. They will if you allow them."

I allowed my uncle to join me and soon he was standing next to me. The Beings of the Light asked me to join our energies together so that he would become a part of me and I would become a part of him. As soon as we merged, they said, "In the Sea of Well-being, you are well. Since you are well and you are your uncle and your uncle is you, then your uncle is well." I could feel the wellness of me and him.

This was healing in the 5th dimension. I also understood that this is how Jesus heals. He sees only wellness and perfection. I understood that if we would only focus on the wellness of things, then that is all we would be able to experience. It is our need to focus on something ill that keeps us experiencing the illness. I also understood that by merging our energies together as one, my uncle and I became one. I was beginning to understand the idea of Oneness.

I was then told that I had just received the Master Healer's Attunement. An attunement is tuning one to a frequency of light that one is not currently readily accessing. If you imagine yourself as a radio and you want to broadcast a certain station, an attunement would put you clearly on that station. Jesus is known as the Master Healer of the Universe, which is why he appeared and administered the attunement process. Please understand that this is not a Christian attunement or an attunement only given to Christians. Sometimes people have difficulty separating Jesus from religion. In truth, Christ's energy is one of the purest, most beautiful lights I have ever encountered and is available to us all regardless of religious belief. Jesus' light is golden and represents the Christ Consciousness or God Consciousness from which we all came. When we wrap ourselves in golden light, we are wrapping ourselves in the Christ Light, or the same light that Jesus carries with him. I am told the color is gold to remind us of our value.

I want to reiterate that the Christ Light is not exclusive. It is readily available to all. There are no requirements to access or receive the Christ Light. You do not have to do, undo, believe, or earn anything. In fact, we each carry the Christ Light within. The attunement reminds us it's there. I have noticed that The Beings of the Light work very closely with Jesus or the Christ Light. It is as if the two energies are kindred spirits.

I asked if this attunement was the same as a Master Level Reiki Attunement. I was told, "No, it is a higher level attunement. It carries a finer vibration than the Master Level Reiki Attunement. The symbols used in this attunement are also different than the symbols used in Reiki." For those who are unfamiliar, Reiki is an ancient form of energy healing that uses symbols and the transmission of the Christ Light to heal. It is very powerful and I recommend finding a Reiki practitioner in your area if you have never experienced it.

My next big question was, "Can I attune others?" The Beings of the Light told me that I could and I would. I was cautioned, however, that this is a high level attunement and when people aren't ready to receive it, they won't. The reason they were telling me this is because I was going to put it into one of my workshops as part of the class. They let me know if people weren't ready to receive the attunement, then they would cancel their registration, and I certainly didn't want that! (Note: If you sign up for spiritual workshops only to find yourself cancelling them, ask yourself if you are sabotaging your own spiritual advancement. Your subconscious mind may be afraid to move forward. Don't let it stop you. If you really want it, push past the fear and go.)

Since I received this attunement, I have attuned a few other people. I have also attuned many things. My house, my car, my furniture, water, my land, my money, and my drum are all examples of some of the things I have attuned to the Master Healer's vibration. In this way, the things around me are emanating the Master Healer's energy of healing. Before attuning any item, I first ask it if it is willing to receive the attunement. If I get a yes, I go ahead with the process. If I get a no, I ask that the thing receive the most beneficial energy for it and all involved to help get it to a level where it will receive the attunement.

If you want to receive the attunement, ask for it, and allow your intuition (imagination) to guide you through imagining the process. If you are ready, you will receive it. If you are asking for it, be honest with yourself and make sure you are ready for it. As always, when you become attuned to higher frequencies, it requires that you release the lower energies that are holding you back. Sometimes this makes life uncomfortable if you resist the letting go process.

If you think you would like to receive this attunement, but think it's not for you because you are not a healer, understand the true definition of a healer. A healer is anyone that shines his light where there is darkness. This means that we all are healers. When we make a sad person smile, we are shining our light. When we laugh and others laugh with us, we are shining our light. When we provide a solution to a problem that previously had none, we are shining our light. As we shine our light, the world becomes a brighter, healthier place. The more we shine, the more we fully step into the shoes of a Master Healer.

Applying the Wisdom

When you are feeling upset and do not know why, sit quietly and allow yourself to feel what you are feeling. When you allow your feelings the opportunity to be felt, you give them permission to tell you why they are present. They aren't there to punish you. They are there to deliver a message. Find out what it is.

Apply love to your feeling by imagining wrapping it in light or showering it and you in a column of golden light. Imagine yourself swimming in the Sea of Well-being. Since the Sea of Well-being is made of light, you don't have to worry about breathing under its waters. You can dive deep down and breathe easily. Feel the wellness.

Invite whatever or whomever you have been viewing as unwell to join you in the Sea of Well-being. Do not leave the Sea of Well-being to go get them. Instead, allow them to join you. When you both are present in the Sea of Well-being, all will feel well. Breathe and let go of any resistance, tension, or fear that you may be feeling. Allow yourself to wade in the wellness. Stay as long as you like.

Repeat this exercise as many times as is necessary until you feel like all will be well.

CHAPTER 14

Fear Flambé

"I never did a day's work in my life. It was all fun." – Thomas Edison

The more I work with The Beings of the Light, the more I trust the Universe to provide. When I have a desire for something to happen, I do not need to know how to make it happen. I know I will be shown the way. It is the way I came up with all the information in this book. It is the way I was shown how to put this book together. The beauty is that sometimes the way comes in the form of help from others who have a desire to give what I wish to receive. Sometimes the way comes in the form of meditations or as ideas that just pop into my head when I'm taking a bath. Sometimes it just happens inexplicably, miraculously, and magically. I have stopped trying to figure out the how and just started enjoying the process. It's just more fun that way. Of course, to get there I had to let go of my beliefs that good has to come from struggle and that hard work is the way to getting ahead. If you're holding onto those beliefs, dump them. It doesn't have to be that way.

As I have stated previously, I have wanted to write a book for a long time. I used to believe that writing a book was going to be a lot of hard work, and that was my experience. I started several books only to have abandoned them because it was too hard. When I finally released the belief that it had to be hard and embraced the possibility that it could be fun, this book appeared and fast. I committed to writing 2000 words a day. When I started, that was a challenge. After a week, 2000 words was easy. The book became a source of fun and excitement to me. Whenever I would worry that I wouldn't be able to have enough material to fill a book, I would affirm that what I didn't know would come to me. And it did. I never was left wondering what to write about. I was given everything I needed when I needed it. For the most part, it was easy.

To be fair, I did more than just decide to change my belief system. The Beings of the Light described to me the full process that I went through. First, I had a strong desire to change the belief that in order for things to happen it had to be hard or had to be a struggle. That desire fed the Universe the order for it to happen. It did not happen as a one-shot deal. Instead, this process occurred for me as a 3-course meal. Each course brought to me in stages, culminating in the most satisfying dessert.

The first course was me asking that all the karmic patterns that encompassed this belief be cleared away. I asked my favorite karmic clearing Archangels, Michael and Raziel, to do this for me. They did. Karma clearing is really that easy. When you believe it can be cleared and ask that it be done, it is just done.

With the karma cleared, my palate was ready for the second course, but I wasn't to dine alone. This particular course was served at our next scheduled Energy Spa Day and The Beings of the Light jokingly named the dish "Fear Flambé."

I remember it well. This particular gathering seemed to have magic wrapped around it. The Beings of the Light told me that the reason the day was so powerful was because we all showed up with the same subconscious desire – to break free of the belief that you had to work hard to get ahead and to replace it with you have to have fun to get ahead.

One of the members of our Energy Spa Day group is a kindred spirit. Like me, he also receives guidance from The Beings of the Light. At this particular gathering, The Beings of the Light instructed him to light a divine fire in which we were to throw the beliefs of hard work to get ahead and anything attached to it. We all could tell exactly where the fire was.

Immediately, we began feeding the fire any and all belief systems holding us back from enjoying prosperity in a fun and easy way. Then, I had the impulse to go stand in the fire. The clairvoyants in the group were amazed at how brightly the fire burned, causing my light to shine brighter. I felt warmer and lighter. It wasn't long before each one of us stood in the divine fire allowing it to burn away any blocks, negativity, or beliefs holding us back from standing in our power. I must admit, for such a light course (no pun intended), I found the Fear Flambé to be absolutely delicious and would highly recommend it to anyone.

Two days after our Energy Spa Day, I was teaching my Advanced Spiritual Techniques class. After the first day of this two-day workshop, I decided to take a walk outside to refresh my energy and connect with nature. Once I left my front door, The Beings of the Light pulled my attention toward the side of my garage where an old wagon wheel was sitting. We inherited the wheel with the house when we bought it. It was one of those old wooden wagon wheels that you would find on the wagons of the old west. This particular wheel was broken. It was more like half of a wagon wheel.

In feng shui terms, the area where the wagon wheel sat was in the career section of my home. My intuition told me to pull it away from the wall. I understood immediately why it could no longer stay there. To me, it represented hardship, effort, and old technology. This is not a good symbol to have sitting in your career section.

Once I pulled the wheel away from the house, I wondered what I should do with it. I dragged it around placing it in various places, but none felt right. I even hurt my back a little dragging it around (it was ridiculously heavy), which served as yet another metaphor of representing back-breaking work and struggle.

I wondered what I should do with it. I started asking questions. Should I keep it? My intuition told me "No." Should I throw it away? "No." Should I recycle it? "No." Frustrated, I asked The Beings of the Light what I should do with it. "Burn it." was the first thing that came to mind. It was a winter day and my fire pit was on the other side of the house. I had no desire to hurt myself further by dragging it to the back of the house. I decided to leave the wheel on the front lawn for now and deal with it in the morning.

The next morning when my students arrived, I told them the story of the wheel. Since part of the learning was for them to access their own intuition, I asked them what messages they were getting about the wheel. Some envisioned pioneers doing hard, back-breaking labor; others saw the broken wheel as something that is no longer working; another heard that it was time to let go of the old and bring in the new. I told them that I had gotten the message to burn it and asked if they would like to take part in a fire ceremony where we would burn it together with the intent to release the belief in things having to be hard in order to move ahead. They eagerly agreed.

Right after lunch, it was time for my third and final course – dessert. The students carried the wheel to the fire pit for me representing to me that help is always available if I would just be patient. To add meaning to our ceremony, we each wrote on a spoke of the wheel with a marker what we wished to release and what we wanted to bring into its place. Even my 8-year-old daughter, who is a very old soul, participated. We burned some sage to purify the space and as an offering to the Universe for granting our requests. Then, we lit the fire. We didn't have much kindling, and the fire was slow at first, but it never went out. We kept saying if the fire went out, we would just keep relighting it to let the Universe know we meant business. The Universe obliged and finally the wheel caught fire. We could feel ourselves getting lighter as it burned away the hardship and the pain that it represented. Best dessert I ever had, and no calories!

The Beings of the Light told me that my young daughter provided a very important presence at the ceremony. She wasn't only there to release the limiting beliefs she held, but also represented the childlike innocence that we had lost as adults and were asking to reclaim. My daughter dropped sweetgrass in the fire and I was told she was asking for the sweetness of life to be brought back to us all in the form of play, fun, and prosperity. She may be only 8, but that is just Earth years. Her soul is pure ancient wisdom. I also find it interesting that the number 8 is the number of prosperity and abundance and is also the infinity symbol turned upright, just adding to the symbolism and magic of the ceremony and making it that much more powerful.

Since that day, things have come to me easier. My workshops seem to fill themselves with no effort on my part. What's also interesting is that I began writing this book two days after that ceremony. I completed it in less than two months. How's that for effortless?

Applying the Wisdom
Lighting the Divine Fire to Burn Away the Unwanted

Ask The Beings of the Light to light the divine fire. It will be lit the moment you ask. Then, imagine your limiting beliefs, blocks, and fears as tangible objects and throw them into the fire. Afterward, stand in the fire or imagine yourself laying in it, allowing it to envelop you. Stay until every last piece of fear has burned away, leaving only shiny, glowing light behind. Breathe deeply and exhale fully. This will help you to release further and more fully. Afterward you should feel lighter and refreshed.

Releasing Ceremony

If you would like to perform your own ceremony, you don't need an old wagon wheel to do it. If you have something that represents the old ways and can be burned, you could use that. Or you simply could write everything you wish to release on one side of a piece of paper. On the other side of the paper, write down what you would like to bring in to replace what will be leaving. After I make a list like this, I always like to add, "this or something better" to allow for outcomes I may not be ready to imagine. Then with trust, focused intent, and belief burn it. It is also always nice to leave an offering as a sign of gratitude. Tobacco is a traditional offering. We used sage and sweetgrass. You can burn incense, sing a song, or play some music. It doesn't matter what it is, as long as it comes from the heart and not out of obligation. You don't have to give anything but feelings of gratitude. It is the gracious acceptance of the magic that is happening that brings the manifestations quicker and purifies the results.

CHAPTER 15

Releasing Suffering

"Although the world is full of suffering, it is full also of the overcoming of it." – Helen Keller

One thing that fills my soul with joy is teaching the techniques I have learned to others so that they may free themselves of what is holding them back. My Advanced Spiritual Techniques workshop is the class where I primarily teach many of the clearing methods I know. One of the methods I teach is how to clear suffering. During one particular class, I had a surprise visitor show up to aid one of the participants in releasing the suffering she was carrying and deliver a very important message to us all.

Just before this visitor's arrival, I had explained to the participants the instructions on how to release suffering. Just as I was going to have them pair up and practice on each other, I felt compelled to add that suffering sometimes shows up as a large wooden cross that a person carries. It is their cross to bear, so to speak, and often feels like an enormous weight on the shoulders. Most people who have a cross to bear are generally not complainers. They feel this is their lot in life - to suffer for their sins.

After I finished explaining this, I realized there was a person in the group who was carrying such a cross. She had come to the workshop to release her guilt over leaving the church and come to terms with her spiritual beliefs, which were different than those she was taught as part of her religion. Like many of us, she was taught that if we didn't follow a certain set of rules and be "good", then we would be punished by God and sent to hell. Even though consciously she understood that God is all-loving and non-judgmental, she still held a subconscious fear that she still may be punished or seen as doing something wrong.

The Beings of the Light showed me how to have her release the suffering and let go of the cross. The first thing I was shown was that the cross was to be placed into a wood chipper until it was completely broken down into wood chips. The wood chips would then be put around trees to serve as mulch. This way the suffering would be transmuted into something useful and loving for the Earth, and she would no longer have to carry it around.

I could tell immediately that the participant was nervous and fearful about letting go of her cross. However, she did like the idea of having it being used for mulch and fostering the growth of trees. As if to answer the questions being formed in her head, I started to receive a clear message, this time not from The Beings of the Light, but from our surprise visitor, Jesus himself.

Jesus told the participant to not bear any cross for his sake. He never wanted anyone to suffer for him. He said what most people do not understand is that he did not suffer on the cross. He was completely at peace. Any suffering people perceived him having was merely a reflection of their own suffering. He said that he does not like the imagery of him nailed to the cross because it perpetuates the idea that we should suffer in his name. Instead, he would like people to replace the image of him on the cross with the Truth of who he is. He showed us how he wanted to be seen. He stood in front of us in robes of white and gold, his hair and skin immaculate, his hands clean and perfect. Beautiful glowing golden light was emanating from his heart and encompassing him so that it was difficult to discern what was his body and what was light. He said, "When you see me, see me as light. When you see me, replace the crown of thorns with a crown of golden light. When you picture me, replace the cuts on my face with a loving glow and the holes in my hands with golden, healing light. No longer picture me in pain or suffering. Picture me only as I am – as perfection, light, and love." And then he said, "And this is how I want you to picture yourself." It brought the participant to tears.

Jesus' message to us that day was very powerful and clear. He no longer wanted people to think they should suffer for his sake. He only wants to be seen as love and for us to see ourselves that way too. No more crosses. No more nails. No more thorns. No more suffering. Just light.

We worked through the exercise and the participant let go of her suffering, bravely placing the cross in the wood chipper, and spreading the mulch around the trees. Jesus was right alongside her the entire time. He joyfully and quite enthusiastically pushed the cross into the wood chipper and happily spread the newly made mulch with her. He was blessing her the entire time and she felt it. Afterward, it was like a dark cloud had been lifted from her. She was smiling and the sadness in her eyes was replaced with a sparkly twinkle. She said she hadn't felt this good since she could remember. When I asked her what picture formed in her mind when I said the word Jesus, she said it was the image of him as the golden, loving light. She no longer associated him with the image of suffering she previously held.

Even as I write this, I feel that beautiful golden light that always is with Christ. Often referred to as the Christ Light or Christ Consciousness in spiritual circles, I have encountered this light often. It has nothing to do with religion. It is non-denominational. It is reserved for no one in particular, available to all, whether the person believes in it or not. It is my favorite light because it carries no judgment. It totally accepts you as you are. It does not care if you made one mistake or ten million. It does not care if you were unloving, nasty, promiscuous, or selfish. It does not care if you are lazy, forgetful, vengeful, depressed, or insecure. It is a light that does not require prerequisites, an entrance exam, or a grade point average. All of those requirements we have created to tell ourselves we are not worthy, not deserving of love, or joy, or pleasure. This light is always the same – golden, pure, powerful, giving, and unconditional. It is love at its purest.

Jesus gave me this message that I will pass on here: "If you see me as suffering on a cross, you are bearing the cross of suffering. It is a reflection of your own personal suffering. Change your perspective of me from one who has been hurt and mistreated to one of love and light. In this way, you will no longer perpetuate the belief that suffering is necessary and focus upon the love that you are. You may wish to replace the crosses you carry around your necks and hang on the wall in your homes with images and symbols of love. You do not dishonor me or your faith by letting go of suffering. It brings me great joy to see you do so. If you feel you must keep the cross, then use it as a symbol of two paths crossing – a crossroads – with every direction leading you to love."

To all those who are reading this, if you feel you are carrying a cross, that a heavy burden is on your shoulders, or that you have done something wrong, please use your imagination and put that cross of suffering in a wood chipper. If it's not a cross, you could gather it up and place it in a cleansing fire and watch it burn to ash. You could have angels bring you a golden garbage can, or garbage truck for that matter, and throw it all away. Let it go to the light. You will be blessed for doing so. Let go of the belief that you are being judged for your sins. You aren't. The only one judging you is you. Judgment is manmade and has nothing to do with the light. God, Jesus, Source, or whatever you want to call it, is not judging you. The light is pure unconditional love. It is loving you, all of you, for all that you are and all that you are not, all of the time.

I know how much it hurts to think that you have to be something other than what you are in order to be loved. I have carried that cross for most of my life and never, ever again will go back to that place. If I can let go of my cross, you can too. Ask Jesus for assistance. He is only too happy to oblige. Consider it you doing your part to help with the environment – the trees are only too happy to accept your wood chips!

Suffering Agreements

Suffering is part of the human condition. Freedom is part of the divine condition. As we continue to free ourselves from the suffering we have taken on, we come closer to our true divine selves. Because suffering is pervasive in our lives, it will take more than putting a cross in a wood chipper to totally eradicate ourselves from it. The cross is just one of many pieces of our suffering. Other forms of suffering will continue to surface as part of our journey, each piece waiting to be freed. This is what spiritual work is, to pursue freedom through the continual release of suffering.

The Beings of the Light showed me in explicit detail the agreements I have subconsciously made to suffer and ways to change those agreements. I share this information with you, because each and every one of us has made agreements with our subconscious on how we are to suffer. By being aware of this information, we then have the power to change it.

When I had finished writing a little over a quarter of this book, I could feel myself beginning to sabotage the process again. I began to feel anxious and afraid that the book wouldn't get published or, if it did, that I would be laughed at or ridiculed for what I was writing. Since I couldn't seem to shake this feeling, I went into a deep meditation asking for help to finally put this issue to rest.

The first thing I was shown was that I was continuing to see the world as an unfriendly place. I asked why I had come back to this perspective. Why hadn't the new perspective of the world I adopted before stayed?

My question was answered with a question. "What if the world was a friendly place?" My inner feeling kept saying, "It's not." Repeatedly I was asked, "What if it was? What if the world was a friendly place? What would that mean for you?"

It was difficult for me to imagine the world as completely friendly, but I allowed my mind to consider the possibility. If the world was a friendly place, then I would feel safe to be me. I would no longer have to hide my feelings or adjust my behavior in order to escape the judgment and ridicule of others. As I began to explore this idea of just being me, I observed myself transforming into an angel with wide expansive wings. When I tried to spread my wings and fly, I found myself caught in a net. I couldn't break free.

The Beings of the Light explained that the net represented the terms and conditions of my suffering agreement. "My suffering agreement? What's that?" I asked.

They explained that a suffering agreement included all the terms and conditions under which I agreed to suffer and how the suffering would be administered. Every person has a suffering agreement, each with different terms and conditions. I was caught in the net, because I was trying to fly by fulfilling my dream of writing and publishing a book on the subject of spirituality. One of the conditions I had agreed to was to keep my light dim. Writing this book was bringing me a great deal of joy and building a confidence and acceptance in who I am. Behavior that invoked such light in me violated the terms of the suffering agreement. I was to invoke suffering to prevent myself from becoming too bright.

I was told, "The good news is that since the suffering agreement is made with the self, it can be changed by the self. It is your own agreement. You can change the terms and conditions anytime you like and in any way you will allow."

I silently affirmed that I wanted to be free of the terms and conditions that were confining me. Immediately, the net holding my wings down began to dissolve into thin air. I spread my wings and began to fly. I left the place where I was being held, the place that I viewed as the unfriendly world, and asked to be directed to the friendly universe. Just ahead, I saw beacons of light. I knew this was the place I wanted to go. Before I arrived I asked that my husband and children join me. I didn't want to go to this place alone. My husband and my oldest daughter appeared and they too, had beautiful wings. When I asked where my youngest was, I immediately got an image of her trapped in a similar net below. It appears this was another term of my suffering agreement. If I were to break free and shine brightly, then one of my children would suffer for it. I immediately asked for this condition and all conditions around my shining brightly be dissolved. My youngest daughter appeared beaming happily and, as a family, we flew to the friendly universe.

As we entered this place of light, an angel greeted us. He welcomed us and said we were welcome to stay. I loved this place and asked my husband if we could move here. He said yes. We asked our children if they would like to live here. They said yes. As a family, we decided to move to this beautiful, friendly place. The angel who greeted us gave us a set of keys signifying that this was now our home and we were free to move in.

The first thing I wanted to do was invite my brothers and sisters to come visit. One by one they came. I asked them to move here too. They said they didn't belong and asked, "What makes you so special to think you belong here?"

The Beings of the Light explained to me that this wasn't actually what my siblings were thinking of me. They reminded me that I was in my subconscious mind, and that in my mind, I was worried that people would ridicule me for being what I wanted to be. My biggest worry was what my family would think of the person I wanted to be – the person that I am. In truth, my siblings hold an enormous amount of love for me.

My siblings were my metaphor for what was going on inside my mind. It was my question, not theirs. "What makes me so special to think that I belong here?" I realized that all the approval I was seeking from them was a representation of my own disapproval of self. I wondered what the best way for me to approve of myself was.

Just then, I was shown myself as a baby. I held my baby self in my arms. I told her that I approved of her and loved her for who she was. She was perfect. She smiled and disappeared as light. In her place was me as a 2 year old. I already was beginning to notice the feelings of disapproval I had for myself. I told my 2 year old self that I was sorry for finding fault with her. I told her she could be who she was, a wise, old soul. Darkness sprung from her and disappeared and she turned into light, leaving behind a light blue crystal. The crystal was placed in my throat chakra, healing it. This kept going on. Younger versions of myself would appear, each one slightly older than the one before. I would approve of all that they were and give them permission to be themselves, then dark would spring from them and disappear leaving light and sometimes a crystal that would be given back to me. This was my process of self-acceptance. I wasn't finished, however.

The next thing I was shown was me, as an adult, in a dungeon. I was sitting on a chair against the wall with a large, rounded ax impaling my chest. I was alive and suffering immensely. The Beings of the Light told me that this was the primary method I used to punish myself. I would slice my heart open with a broad, rounded ax. They told me that I had made this part of my suffering agreement.

I knew I was hard on myself, but this? Yet, I could feel the truth of it. This is what it felt like whenever I felt I had disappointed someone, made someone angry, or done something wrong – a blade straight through the heart.

I walked over to myself and removed the ax. I told my slain self that I loved her and that she would suffer no more. I held the ax and felt its cool steel. I told the ax that it would never again have to inflict harm on another person. It seemed to thank me for being relieved of its duties. I asked that any pain that it caused under my bidding, be released and all wounds be healed with loving light. The ax then began to glow golden light and in a flash disappeared. In its place sat a feather pen. A Being of the Light picked up the pen and motioned for my now healed self to sit at a desk and begin writing.

The Beings of the Light told me that while this part of myself sat at the desk and wrote freely, I must come with them to dissolve the secondary sources of suffering that were still active in my suffering agreement.

The next image I saw was me burning at the stake. I immediately threw a bucket of water on the fire, untied my tortured self, and brought me off the stake. I told my tortured self that I loved her and this would no longer happen. I went to the fire, where the dowsed flames had once again started to burn. I told the fire that I would no longer use it to allow myself to be burned, but instead use it with love to cleanse, warm, and add light to the world. The fire thanked me. I asked that all burns I had received by the use of fire be healed, and like a phoenix that springs from the ashes, may the wounds allow for blessings and love to be reborn.

I went to the stake and told it I would no longer use stakes to inflict pain. Instead, I would throw them in the fire where they could provide warmth and fuel for heating. The stake thanked me. I placed the stake in the fire and felt the warmth of it. I asked that all stakes that have brought me pain be placed into the cleansing fire to provide warmth and fuel. I also asked for any pain caused by the stakes to be healed with pure light leaving love in its place.

I went to the ropes that tied my hands and feet. I have felt the suffering of rope many times in my life. Often I have felt my hands were tied or that a rope was wrapped around my neck. I told the rope that I would no longer use it to tie myself up or hang myself. The rope thanked me. I asked that all rope serve the purpose to help, not harm. The rope formed itself into the image of a rope bridge and told me it was safe to cross it. The bridge took me away from the Land of Suffering into the Land of Love. I asked that all the rope that had been used to hold myself back, hang, or hurt myself, be now used to make bridges to beautiful places and that all the suffering it may have caused be released forever more.

The Beings of the Light said there was one more component to this healing process. I was to balance the elements within. We had already balanced the fire element by removing the need to use it to cause pain and honoring its use in the name of the light: to light, to cleanse, to warm, and to transmute.

The next element to balance was water. In the dark, water is used to drown. The water element is unbalanced if you feel like you're drowning and can't come up for air. In the name of the light, water is used to cleanse, dissolve darkness, flow, and hydrate. I asked that in all instances where I used water to drown that light be restored allowing the water to act in the way it was originally intended.

Next, we worked with the element of air. Air is meant to be inhaled and exhaled in a balanced equation of giving equals receiving. In the dark, air builds up without being exhaled creating pressure. This may be prevalent for you if you are feeling like you are full of hot air or like you're going to explode. In the light, air allows you to breathe, receive through inhalation, give through exhalation, and bring forth new possibility on the winds of change. I asked that all instances where my air element was causing me to hold my breath and to feel pressured be changed to allow me to breathe easily, become inspired, give freely from my heart, and bring forth new possibilities.

The next element that was to be balanced was the earth element. In the dark, earth suffocates and traps you. This may be prevalent for you if you feel you're being buried alive or are stuck in the mud. In the light, earth is a fertile field that provides a place for growth, nurtures a crop, and grounds. I imagined all areas of my earth element being loosened and prepared for seeding. I asked that any instance of earth causing feelings of being buried alive or being stuck be replaced with feelings of growth, nurturing, and grounding.

The last element The Beings of the Light wanted to address was the element of metal. My knowledge of the elements had come from the shamanic teachings. In shamanism, there are four elements. I was surprised to hear we would be working with a fifth. I had not worked with this element before. The Beings of the Light told me that in the dark the element of metal cuts, binds, and imprisons. Think of swords, shackles, and jails with their iron bars. I asked why this element was not addressed in shamanism. They told me that shamanic teaching was established well before the use of metal for weapons, prisons, and shackles. Their teachings are based on love and freedom. Metal was not an issue to them. Certainly there were arrowheads, but even they were used only in ceremony to hunt to feed the tribe. It was all done in honor. In the early establishment of the shamanic wisdom, the metal element never needed addressing, because it was never out of balance. Not so, anymore.

They told me if I wanted to fit metal into the shamanic teachings, here is how I would do it. Each element, earth, fire, air, and water corresponds to a direction, north, south, east, and west. Metal would correspond to the center, the light within, where all our strength lies.

The Beings of the Light informed me that my metal element was way out of balance. I had used metal to cut, bind, and imprison me for lifetimes. It was time to see metal for its true purpose. In the light, metal nourishes, fortifies, and strengthens. All the minerals in our body are metals – zinc, iron, and magnesium to name a few. These metals help keep our bones strong, fortifying our skeleton. Our inner metal, therefore, corresponds to our inner strength. When our inner metal is in balance, we are strong; therefore, we don't need to protect ourselves with plates of armor or build weapons to keep the enemy at bay. Some people feel so unsafe that they wall themselves up with plates of armor only to find themselves trapped in a prison of their own making. Some people, like me, use the strength of metal to hold themselves back by shackling their hands and feet and throwing away the key or to cut themselves down to size, keeping one smaller than they really are. If you view metal in the dark, it is harmful. It only makes sense that you would be afraid to unleash the full power of your metal for fear of hurting someone. In the light, however, unleashing the full power of your metal allows you to be who you are – a loving, powerful, strong light that fortifies and strengthens all that you touch.

It was time to throw off the shackles and see metal as friend instead of foe. I told the metal I wore as shackles that I would now allow it to shine in the light and strengthen me. The shackles seemed to smile and began glowing. They sprung open and dissolved into light. As they did so, my inner light began to shine brighter. I asked all superfluous metal in my body to return to the earth. I felt the heavy metals in my body drain into the earth and also nourish my own earth element providing a richer soil for my inner garden. I asked that all metal that I allowed to cut, wound, or torture me in any way be relieved of those duties and transformed into the light of inner strength as is intended. I felt old hurts mending and a deeper sense of love and gratitude than I had ever felt previously. I felt the pain in my heart that I had grown accustomed to carrying around with me lessen, and be replaced with love – strong, arduous, confident love.

Since this experience, I cannot say that I am totally free of suffering and I am not sure I ever will be. What I can say is that I am much kinder to myself and feel better overall. The pain I feel in the low times is not as intense as it previously was and my good moods are more enjoyable and last longer. I do not feel as much fear around the idea of being me. This is the beauty of this work. It makes life better. The thing to remember is that it can always get better. We are infinite in our ability to shine, and like infinity, this journey has no end.

Applying the Wisdom

The Beings of the Light asked me to share this experience with you because it is their desire to have each and every one of you become aware of and dissolve the terms and conditions of your own personal agreement of suffering. Understand that, like the journey that has no end, this is an ongoing process that may need to be revisited from time to time.

Sit quietly and relax while you breathe slowly and deeply. Ask The Beings of the Light to show you the terms and conditions of your suffering agreement and follow their guidance. If you are unsure of the information you are receiving, you may use my own account as a template. Notice where your wings are held captive and ask that the terms and conditions of your agreement be dissolved in order to allow you to fly. Ask what your methods of torturing yourself are and undo them. Balance all five elements within you, just through your intention to do so and pay attention to the metaphors that come to mind if you were to describe them. What resonates as true for you? Perhaps you don't cut yourself down to size but instead whip yourself into submission. Take that whip and relieve it of its duties to cause pain. If you are carrying a cross, chuck it into the wood chipper. Use your imagination. It will tell you what you need to know. Trust the information you are getting. You will know if something is true the moment you hear, see, feel, or sense it. This is your intuition's way of talking to you, through your senses and especially through your ability to sense resonance. If it strikes a chord, then it's true. If it feels out of key, then it's off. You know. How do you know? You sense the resonance. This has nothing to do with your musical ability. I may sing off key, but my sense of feeling is always in perfect pitch. So is yours.

Your imagination is not some silly thing that was only useful when you were a kid and inappropriate for you as an adult. Your imagination is your gateway to the magic of the 5th dimension and the key to accessing the wonderful world and perhaps not so wonderful world you have created in your subconscious mind. Any change in that world begins in the mind. The only way to get there is through your imagination. Go there often. You will reap the most reward by consciously using your imagination to create the changes that you want. It is time.

It is important to know that when the subconscious mind decides to suffer, it does not decide to suffer for a finite period of time. Instead, it decides to suffer for eternity. Either you suffer or you don't. I haven't met one person who isn't suffering in one way or another. The important thing to remember is that it is our decision to stop it. It can help the subconscious mind to tell it you are releasing the suffering in this dimension of time, in all dimensions of time, in all lifetimes, for all eternity, now. This phrasing encompasses every possible moment and lets the subconscious mind know you cannot delay the suffering by placing it in the future or keep actively reminding you of the past. You are telling the mind the suffering is gone now and forever.

Using the metaphors that your mind gives you to illustrate your suffering, change the picture to one where you are free of the pain and responsibility. Give it all away to the light. If you get stuck as to what to do, ask the angels, The Beings of the Light, or Jesus to help you. Allow them to show you what to do next. They will. Keep working with the mind's imagery until it is totally changed to something beneficial when you think of it. Your feelings should also match the imagery, meaning that when you think of the issue you should feel good about it and no longer feel like you are in a place of suffering.

CHAPTER 16

An Audience with the Pope

"That's me in the spotlight, losing my religion." – REM

I was not able to follow a spiritual path without taking time to define my own truth about what God is and my connection to him. I have found this to be especially important for anyone who was raised in a religion that left one feeling incomplete or unfulfilled. I have realized, if you don't get straight on what you believe regarding God and religion, whatever that is, it will be impossible to find out the truth of who you are.

I want to say I have nothing against religion. I know that for many people the choice to follow a religious faith brings them hope, community, trust, and solace. If the practice of your religion provides these things for you, I am very happy for you, and honor your choice in every way. However, religion has not provided these things for me. Instead, religion has left me feeling guilty, confused, wrong, and judged. For these reasons, I have chosen to let it go to follow my own heart and come to know God in my own way.

I was baptized, took communion, and confirmed in the Roman Catholic Church. Whether I was taught this or not, I summarized God as judgmental and punishing. I believed I had better tow the Catholic line or else burn in hell. As I came into my late teens and entered university, my beliefs were challenged when I attended a Religious Studies course and learned the history behind the Roman Catholic Church. I learned of the corruption, the dogma, and the manmade rules that had nothing to do with the Bible. It was such a relief. Many of the rules that I had been taught went against what I truly believed in my heart. When I was 16, I remember feeling guilty and angry for being forced to sign a petition against abortion, a subject about which I was not sure how I truly felt. I remember the first time I had sex (out of wedlock, of course) and afterward feeling like I had somehow dug my own grave. I remember getting my first prescription for birth control using the argument, if I'm going to sin once by having sex outside of marriage, I might as well sin twice by taking birth control and avoid getting pregnant. I remember the first time I attended confession and making up sins because I couldn't think of anything I may have done wrong except fight with my brothers and sisters. And I remember the priest assigning me prayers to say in order to atone for my sins, and not knowing what the prayers were, and being scared that I would be punished for not knowing them. I still don't know the Act of Contrition. In any case, that Religious Studies course opened my eyes and gave me permission to think for myself. I decided that I truly did not believe in the Roman Catholic dogma and rules, and no longer would consider myself Roman Catholic.

Easier said than done.

I joined the military. They asked what religion I wanted put on my dog tags. Mine said, "RC". I had reconstructive knee surgery and the hospital asked to state my religion on the admittance form. I put "RC" (and then I was annoyed when a nun showed up to pray with me). By the time it came time for me to be married, I was relieved to find out that my husband had not been baptized, which apparently is a requirement to be married in the Catholic Church. I really didn't want to be married in the Catholic Church. We were married in a United Church instead. The truth was there was still a subconscious hold on me to be attached to a church, even if I had no desire to attend one or believe in the rules they professed around God being a punishing God.

I decided it was time for me to make up my own mind about God and religion. I asked for guidance and I got it. All paths led to the same answer: God is love and God is infinite. I am a child of God; therefore, I am love and I am infinite. My guidance also led me to the belief that all judgment is manmade. All suffering and punishment is manmade. God is unconditional love, plain and simple. Any suffering or strife is not an act of God, but rather a disconnection from God, from Source, from the Universal Energy that is God, the Creator, the Universe, or whatever you would like to call it. It is a disconnection from love. These beliefs deeply resonated with me and have become the dogma from which I live my life.

I came to the conclusion that a loving God does not care if I am a churchgoer or not. A loving God loves absolutely without conditions. Any lack of love or judgment I feel is my disconnecting from that Source of Love, and not a punishment for not being good enough.

I thought I had finally made peace with my idea of God and my decision to leave the Roman Catholic Church. That is, until the fall of 2011, when my mother died.

My mother's funeral was held at our local Catholic Church. It was a beautiful funeral and the priest did a lovely job honoring my mother in his sermon. When it came time for people to go up to partake in communion, I felt oddly compelled to go. It is not that I wanted communion. It was not that I felt I needed it. After careful reflection, I realized I took the communion because I felt it was expected of me. Clearly there was still some strange force holding me to the Catholic tradition that I could not understand. Trust me, there was no outside pressure – no one pushing me out of a pew to get up there. This was totally an inside job.

That night, before I went to sleep, I tried to understand the feelings I had regarding this scenario. I realized that every time I entered a Catholic mass I felt great angst and a compulsion to go receive communion. It was not a pleasant experience and I never felt better after receiving the communion. I just felt more of the proverbial Catholic guilt. I asked my higher guidance for clarity around this issue and fell asleep.

I woke up the next morning in a meditative state. The Beings of the Light were informing me that the reason I was having difficulty separating myself from the Church was because of many vows I had taken in the Catholic Church in previous lives. In order for me to move forward on my journey, these vows would need to be broken.

Just then, Pope John Paul II appeared to me. This was quite shocking to me. It's not often you get a private audience with the pope, even if it is posthumously. He informed me he was there to grant me absolution. He showed me a line of swords that represented all of the vows I had made to the Catholic Church. He then proceeded as follows:

"I now hereby absolve you from all vows that you have made to the Catholic Church. You are absolved from any pain and suffering these vows may have caused you. You are absolved from all guilt taken on as a result of making these vows. You are absolved from any responsibility or obligation that you have unduly taken on as a result of making these vows. You are absolved from any persecution or judgment you may have received as a result of taking these vows. You are absolved from the need to punish yourself or do penance as a result of any instance of breaking these vows. And, (the show-stopper) you are absolved from ever having to be Catholic again."

As soon as he said the last sentence, the swords began snapping in front of me, breaking into tiny pieces. Pieces of parchment sprung from some of the swords that were gathered into a pile. I was told these were contracts I had signed in blood that needed to be destroyed. Archangel Michael appeared. He pierced the entire pile with his sword of light causing the contracts to burst into flames, rendering them null and void. By the time it was all over, I felt like a huge weight was being lifted from my body and replaced with a sense of freedom I had long awaited. I thanked Pope John Paul II for his grace and he nodded with a smile saying he was very thankful to have given it.

When I finally got out of bed, I felt light and energized. Oddly, that morning I came across a rosary that I had kept in my possession for years. It had no sentimental value to me. I just was never able to throw it away. That morning, I looked at it and knew immediately I no longer needed it. Just like the swords, I broke it into little pieces and gladly threw it away, knowing I no longer had any unwanted binding attachment to the Church. I felt free and more love in my heart than I had ever felt before.

The Beings of the Light communicated with me that morning after the absolution. They told me that I was given an important piece of healing knowledge that I could use with others. The knowledge was how to effectively eradicate past and present life vows that were no longer serving a person's better good.

I had been aware of the non-beneficial effects of past life vows from my previous spiritual training. I had also been aware of how difficult it could be to totally eradicate the vows because of their strong hold on people. It takes more than confidently affirming, "I break this vow now." to release the hold it has on you.

The Beings of the Light told me that it is important to receive absolution from the authority to which the vow was made. The Pope represented the Head of the Church and was the authority from which my subconscious mind and cellular memory needed absolution in order to be freed. They also told me that no authority can deny absolution when asked for it.

They continued to tell me that once vows are broken, written contracts will often appear and that they need to be cleared and voided. Archangel Michael stabbed the papers that appeared before me with his sword of light to "take the air out of them", much like taking the air out of a tire rendering it useless. The contracts then were destroyed by a cleansing fire, eradicating them from existence.

The final step was to fill my body with light filling in any voids or spaces left from the departing vows and contracts. I was told that The Beings of the Light did this for me and that is when I felt the feeling of freedom and lightness.

I have used this technique ever since with clients and have eradicated various vows including past life vows of poverty, chastity, pestilence, suffering, obedience, silence, penance, and retribution. I have even used it to eradicate present life marriage vows that were causing issue in a client who had been divorced. Because she had vowed to "love, honor, and cherish until death do us part" and her ex was still alive, she was unable to move forward with her life. When we broke the marriage vow, she felt relief and a sense of freedom from her ex-husband. Other vows that I have cleared are vows to do better or be better, which cause a feeling of never doing or being enough and vows of hiding who you truly are. Once broken, the client feels instantly relieved and is able to move forward fearlessly.

I now am very careful with the language 'I vow that…" I don't want to create a situation that may cause me suffering in my next life! I now use the phrasing "I intend that…" This way I can reap the benefits of my intention in the moment and avoid non-beneficial, unforeseen consequences in the future.

Applying the Wisdom

If there is something holding you back that you just can't seem to get past, it may be a vow or series of vows. If you receive your intuition through feeling, like me, a vow feels like a strong pull in the body that can't be broken. Whenever you come across this feeling, you likely have a vow or a series of vows to break.

Ask The Beings of the Light to assist you in calling in all authorities you made these vows to and require absolution from. They will just show up. Understand that you do not need to know who the authorities are. They know. Just ask for them to show up and become aware of their presence. Then, allow yourself to hear, feel, see, or know that from which they are absolving you. Normally they will absolve you from all the conditions of the vow and any pain and suffering you have taken on as a result of making the vow. Once the absolution has been given imagine the vows as broad swords lined up in a row. There may only be one sword or many. Confidently affirm, "I break these vows now!" and notice how the swords snap and break as you do. If they do not snap, you have not broken the vow. Ask for more guidance as how to get the sword to snap. Pay attention to see if any contracts spring forth from the swords. These will need to be destroyed. Ask Archangel Michael to render any contracts void, burn them, and to replace what leaves with light.

If you are harboring guilt from leaving your religious faith to follow a spiritual life or a life of your own choosing, ask the head of the church and God himself to appear to you to provide you with absolution. They will. Break any vows and agreements as necessary. I must say that Pope John Paul II absolving me from my ties to the church has been one of the most powerful and freeing things that I have experienced on my spiritual journey. It can be that way for you too.

Vow breaking is a very powerful, healing process, and well worth the time it takes in meditation to do it. Just know that you can. Do not be afraid to try. If you call in the help of The Beings of the Light and the angels, you will be guided. Trust you know what to do. What you don't, you will be shown and intuitively guided. It may be just what you need in order to leap forward on your path.

CHAPTER 17

The One Who Held My Heart

"He sounds perhaps like an illusion…Illusions are dangerous people; they have no flaws." – Fanny Ardant as Irene in the motion picture Sabrina

I know from my spiritual training that if a person from the past keeps entering your thoughts, then you likely have unfinished business with them. This doesn't mean you have to find them to finish what is undone. Most often, you can come to a place of peace by going within and facing the truth of why that person is still there. There is always a reason and you may be surprised by what it is.

My mind kept going back to a person from my past. I couldn't seem to shake him out of my thoughts. I thought I was long done with him, but there he was. I knew there had to be a reason he was still there. What was I hanging onto? What was it that I still needed to learn?

When I was in my twenties I met a man who I came to very much love and, he too, very much loved me. Due to long distance and other circumstances not under our control, we were not able to have a traditional relationship. Over the course of five years, we met perhaps a handful of times. While our time together was brief, it was heartfelt, passionate, real, and respectful.

It was a strange relationship unlike any other I ever had. I never expected anything from this man. I never expected him to break ties or uproot his life to be with me. The only thing I wanted was for him to truly be happy. This was certainly not the way I felt or acted with other boyfriends. I think this must be what unconditional love is. Not needing the person to fill some void in you and make you happy, but instead, loving him completely for who he is and wishing him happiness even if he's not meant to be with you. This is how I felt about this person. The only reason our communication finally ended is because I met someone else. When I told him I was engaged to be married, he left me alone to build my life with my soon to be husband. He didn't want to get in the way of our relationship. He, too, wanted only for me to be happy. We understood that our time together was perfect and its natural end was the way it was meant to be.

As I reflected on my thoughts about him, I realized that in my mind, I had made him my back-up plan. If anything were to happen to my husband, he was my subconscious mind's answer to not being alone. Consciously, this made no sense. For one, I didn't know how to contact him anymore. Two, I doubt he is single and available to be my back-up; and three, even in the unlikely event of my needing a back-up and he being available, I knew we wouldn't make a good fit long term. I'm quite certain things would not be good between us in a traditional relationship, because we had wanted different things from life.

Still, I wasn't able to get him out of my mind. He would enter my thoughts and I would obsess about him and create all sorts of "what if" scenarios. This was becoming annoying to me, because it takes time to obsess about someone and, most importantly, I didn't even want a relationship with this man. The relationship with my husband was and is the most important relationship to me. We have a good, strong marriage. Why did this man from my past keep showing up? And why did I need a back-up plan?

As I began to ask and reflect as to the reason he kept popping into my thoughts, I realized I didn't feel secure on my own. The thought of being separated from my husband left me feeling lost and helpless. It seems I have spent my whole life trying to find someone to love me. If my husband died, who would do that? I needed this man from my past to be my back-up because I knew he loved me. What I hadn't considered up until this point was that I could be the one to love me. I could be my back-up plan.

In order to foster this feeling of self-love, The Beings of the Light began working with my inner child. They asked me to imagine myself as a little girl. I pictured myself around the age of four. They then asked me to ask her what it was that she needed. There was so much that she needed. She needed to feel loved, to feel lovable, to feel important, and to feel valued. Then, The Beings of the Light sent angels to bring in love beams carrying the light of all these things that I and my four-year-old self needed. As I imagined that light entering our bodies, my feelings of insecurity began to vanish. Still, there was something missing.

The Beings of the Light then asked me to think of someone or something I loved unconditionally. I immediately thought of my daughters. They asked me to feel the unconditional love I had for my daughters in my heart. I did. Then they asked me to look at my inner child and transfer those feelings of unconditional love I had for my daughters to her. I was to feel the same way about my inner child as I did about my daughters.

This immediately brought me to tears. In this one simple exercise, The Beings of the Light had showed me how I had been denying myself love. At first it was difficult to feel the same way about my inner child as I did about my daughters. I felt like she (I) didn't deserve that kind of love. The Beings of the Light talked me through it. They said, "You are four years old. You are even younger than your daughters. What could you possibly need to do in order to deserve love? You are innocent. You are pure. This is a girl who deserves love, just as all children deserve love. You have the power to give it to her and we are telling her that she has the power to give it to herself. Stop denying yourself the love you deserve. Stop denying that child the love she deserves. Allow that love to come in now. Allow yourself to let it in. No more conditions. No more rules. That little girl gets whatever she wants now without needing a reason. Give her whatever she wants. Give her what she needs."

As they spoke, their words hit home. I could no longer deny myself the love that I had been expecting someone else to provide. I didn't need it from someone else because I had it within me the entire time. I was just keeping it locked outside my door. When I opened that door and let the love in, everything changed. I felt full, confident, and complete. I felt loved.

Now, that I had met my needs for love, I tested myself to see if I had fixed my issue with this man from the past. I thought about him and still he seemed to linger in my thoughts. My thoughts had changed, however. I knew I would be ok if I suddenly found myself alone. I knew I no longer needed him to be my back-up plan. But something was still calling me to him.

I tried all the spiritual tricks in my arsenal. I cut energy cords and cleared karma. I even asked other energy workers to disconnect us. Nothing seemed to work. It was time to go right to the source and talk to this man from my past face-to-face. In my next meditation, that's exactly what I did. I imagined him in front of me and told him everything I could think of to say. I told him how I treasured our time together. I told him how I loved how his eyes lit up whenever I entered a room. I told him how I felt like the most important person in the room when he was there. I told him that I was happily married to a wonderful, kind man and we had two beautiful daughters. I told him that I had him in my thoughts so very much lately and that it needed to stop so that I could focus my energies on my marriage and family. I told him that I was sorry things didn't work out for us to be together in this life, but that it was exactly what it was supposed to be. I told him once again how my greatest wish was for him to be happy and have a joyful life, and that he needed to find that without me in it, just as I needed to find my happiness without him in it. I told him I loved him, but that I needed to say goodbye. He smiled at me, nodded, and from behind his back, he produced a black box tied with a red ribbon and placed it on the ground in front of me. He backed away, turned, and left.

The Beings of the Light appeared and I asked them to open the box that lay at my feet. Inside, there was a glowing red item. I couldn't quite distinguish what it was. The Beings of the Light carefully pulled the item from the box and I was shocked by what I saw. It was an almost whole, human heart. I recognized it instantly. This wasn't just any heart; this was my heart.

The Beings of the Light carefully placed the heart back into my body. Feelings of joy, freedom, and love overcame me. I asked how the man from my past had gotten my heart. They replied, "You gave it to him. You gave it to him for safekeeping. And we must say, he did a wonderful job. He kept your heart in perfect condition never allowing anyone to utter a bad word or harsh judgment about you in his presence. While in his care, he loved, nurtured, and protected your heart. He agreed to do this for you until you were able to do it for yourself. When you spoke to him honestly about your feelings, he knew you were ready to take your heart back. This is why he gave it to you."

They continued to speak. "Did you ever wonder why you two had such a perfect, untainted relationship without any arguments and petty judgments? Did you ever wonder why he came into your life in such a way that it was impossible for you two to ruin your love for each other? As you already know, you were not meant to spend time as husband and wife or as significant others. He came into your life to keep your heart safe and remind you of who you truly are. In return, you reminded him of who he truly is. You gave him the greatest gift a man can receive – an opportunity to love, honor, and respect the divine feminine. You helped him understand what it is to be a man. And he helped you understand what it is to be a woman.

"We must tell you that you have learned another important tool that you can use in your healing sessions with others. What you just experienced was akin to a soul fragment retrieval, except in this case, it was not the soul that was fragmented and retrieved; it was the heart."

I had performed many soul fragment retrievals with clients in private sessions. Essentially, in times of trauma or stress, the soul can fragment and be left in the hands of another person or even just be caught in limbo somewhere. Often people will describe a soul fragment as losing a little piece of themselves. Sometimes they will refer to a traumatic event and say a little part of them died that day. The little part of them that felt like it died is actually the describing of a soul fragmentation. Soul fragments are not always related to trauma. We will give a piece of our soul away in hopes to get someone to love us or do something for us we don't think we can do for ourselves. This is akin to selling our soul. But you need not worry. The soul cannot be owned by another person, it can only be given on temporary loan. Sometimes, we will exchange soul pieces through the act of sexual intercourse. This is why someone who has had multiple partners will often feel lost, or not whole. They need their soul pieces back. Luckily, it is very easy to retrieve them.

To retrieve a soul fragment, you simply ask for a representative of the Light such as Archangel Michael, The Beings of the Light, or your higher guidance to retrieve the missing fragment and bring it home. Through this process, the fragment will be restored to its original perfection, and placed back into your heart, where it will find its way home. With this practice, it is prudent to check to see if an exchange is necessary. You may be holding onto soul fragments that do not belong to you. Ask that any fragments that belong to others be returned in pristine condition. This will be done upon request.

When I learned the soul retrieval/soul exchange techniques, others around me spoke of how amazing they felt and how it deeply affected them. I did not have this reaction. I felt very little. It wasn't until I received my heart back from the man from my past that I experienced the feelings that my classmates had described. The Beings of the Light informed me that I had many more heart fragments in need of retrieval than soul fragments. That, and it is difficult to feel joy without your whole heart present.

I understood what they meant when they said I had more heart fragments that needed retrieving than soul fragments. After my return from our family vacation in Hawaii, I was feeling odd, not myself, like something was missing. I asked a friend who also does this work what was going on. She said, "You left something in Hawaii. What did you leave there?" Instantly, I knew the answer.

"My heart." I really loved the time I spent in Hawaii. She laughed and said, "Well take it back. The message is you don't need to leave your heart behind to let someone or something know you love it." After I took my heart back, which I now know was a heart fragment, I instantly felt better.

The reason I was fragmenting my heart was that I had a belief that if I loved something I had to give up a piece of myself to let it know. This knowledge made me realize that I had left pieces of my heart all over the place. I had heart fragments left with my dad, my husband, my children, my brothers and sisters, my cat, past lovers, aunts, uncles, friends, and places that I had visited. I began taking them all back. It was like love overload. The wonderful after effect of this was that I had an even greater capacity to love. I finally had enough of my heart back to truly open up to my husband like I always wanted, but was never really able to before. I felt more love for my children, my siblings, for everything! It was truly miraculous.

I gave up the belief that I had to give away a piece of myself in order to love someone and replaced it with a new belief: in order to love someone or something, I must carry that love in my heart. This way I stay responsible for that love and am able to nurture it. If I give it away, I am unable to allow that love to grow. Like pulling a plant from its roots stops the ability for the plant to grow, my fragmenting my heart was stopping my ability to allow my love to grow. I was leaving it in other people's and place's hands. I was sticking my plants in their gardens. Only problem was, their gardens may not be the right soil for my plants, and they had their own plants to look after. Obviously, this was not serving them or me.

The Beings of the Light say that holding onto soul and heart fragments is like taking on responsibility for another because the person in question does not feel confident to do for him or herself. While done with good intentions, thinking we are helping, this act can be disempowering. I gave my heart to the man from my past and he agreed to take on the responsibility of keeping my heart safe. This was done in love, but was still disempowering. As long as he held my heart, I was unable to take responsibility for loving myself. I gave that responsibility to him. He did a good job, but still left me feeling lost without him. I needed to take my heart back in order to truly feel fulfilled and have the capacity to love others as I wished. The man from my past was not able to do that for me. I am the only one that can fill that job.

When we give fragments of our heart or soul to another, it is a way of attaching ourselves to them. Attachments, even those made in love, can be limiting. When we attach to something, we are not free from it. Our whole inner being is based on freedom. Attachments weigh us down and make our inner being feel trapped. Take time to notice where you may have attachments. They are commonly found within parent-child, supervisor-subordinate, teacher-student, girlfriend-boyfriend, and husband-wife relationships. While you may tell yourself you are helping and being kind by taking responsibility for or doing for someone else, know it is far more loving and empowering to allow someone to do for themselves. It also frees you to do for yourself instead of spending your energy on someone else's wishes. Just like the mama bird that must push her babies out of the nest, so must we learn to fly for ourselves and allow others to fly for themselves.

The Beings of the Light say they would rather see people release the responsibility they have taken on than hang onto it in suffering. By releasing responsibility of others and allowing yourself instead to love and care for them from a place of heart, one provides a greater service to all involved. This allows the person or thing you care for to grow and develop on its own, instead of under your control. For the people who read this that describe themselves as control freaks, this is a big step for you. Your needing to control is a result of your attachment. Most of the attachment tends to be to outcome. The irony is, if you would detach, the outcome would be more to your liking and come with much less effort. If you detach and the outcome is not to your liking, then it was never yours to develop in the first place.

I now always check for possible missing heart fragments with my clients and it never ceases to amaze me how freeing and healing this process is. By taking ownership of one's heart and soul, one must detach from the disempowering connection we have made with others. It is truly healing for both parties.

I no longer have or feel the need to create a new back-up plan. I know that if things should change in such a manner that I am left without my wonderful husband, then I shall move forward knowing a greater love will present itself when the time is right. This is immensely comforting to me. It also explains why I used to worry that my husband was going to die prematurely. Anytime he would come home ten minutes late I would be working myself into a tizzy wondering if I should call the hospitals. This was the work of my inner child worried that no one would be around to love her. Not so anymore.

Since receiving my heart fragment back from the man from my past, I have not once obsessed or felt compelled to spend large parts of time thinking about him. He does enter my mind from time to time, but only for a moment, only long enough to say thank you and wish him well. I leave this message in this book to that man:

"I doubt you will ever come to read this my dear friend, but if you do, I want you to know I am very grateful to you and the part you have played in my life. And while you may no longer carry a piece of my heart with you, please know that there is always a place in my heart for you. I wish you love, health, and happiness, and all things magically wonderful."

Another Missing Piece

It wasn't the last time I was to see imagery of my heart hidden away. When I was 65% through writing this book, I felt the ideas drying up. I knew I wasn't finished and that there was more to come, but was at a loss as to what to write next.

I sat quietly with my eyes closed and asked where the rest of the information for my book was located. I immediately imagined myself in a hallway that had one door at the end, and one door perpendicular. Both doors were locked. I knew the information I needed was behind one of those doors. I saw myself banging on the doors asking for them to open. The more I banged the more frantic I became. I began talking to my frantic self and telling her to calm down. I assured her that everything was going to be ok. She didn't seem to be listening. I called on The Beings of the Light for help.

I heard them whisper, the key to what you want is inside. I took a moment to look inside myself and immediately saw a large vault. I had the key for the vault in my hand. I opened the vault and out popped another vault, this one smaller and more ornate than the one before it. The same key unlocked this vault. Inside of it was another vault, similar but just a little smaller than the one before. The same key fit into the lock, and inside was another vault. It was like a set of Russian dolls that open only to find a slightly smaller version inside. The problem was that the smaller versions never seemed to end. They just kept jumping out of the vault that came before it. I realized this was a never-ending loop. The Beings of the Light told me it was a magic box I had created to distract me from finding what I was looking for. It was designed to send me on an endless journey of seeking without finding. Why would I want to distract myself from finding information for a book? I was confused. I tapped the never-ending opening vaults with a magic wand and made them vanish.

When I looked back, the original vault that I had opened was still there. I noticed there was something in it. I reached in and pulled out a book. Could it be my book? I took out the volume. It was covered in dust and the ends of the pages were tattered. It looked very old. It was leather bound, and I could tell it contained the truth. I brought the book up to my chest to allow its wisdom to enter my heart and become part of me. As I allowed the book in, the two doors in the hallway opened.

The opening to the door located at the end of the hallway shone brightly with light. It shone so brightly that I couldn't see what was inside. I knew it was light, but I felt if I entered it, I would be trapped in a closet. I didn't want to go in. The opening to the second door was completely black, yet it felt oddly familiar. It felt like this opening would lead somewhere. It didn't make me feel trapped like the other door. Which door to choose? I knew I needed to take the one with the light, even though I was scared. I asked The Beings of the Light for help and noticed my guardian angels appearing beside me holding my hands.

The angels motioned me to the light-filled doorway. Taking a deep breath, I stepped over the threshold and into the space. Just as I had expected, it was a tiny closet-like room. The angels told me to bring my awareness up. As soon as I did, I was transported out of the constricting closet and into freedom. I had found the way out.

The Beings of the Light appeared again and said now was the time for me to open the book I had placed inside my heart. As I opened it, a box popped out of it. The Beings of the Light opened the box and inside was another very large human heart. "Is that my heart?" I needn't have asked. I knew it was. But I was confused. I thought I had gotten my heart out of the box when I said goodbye to the man from my past. The Beings of the Light told me that the man from my past held one aspect of my heart. This was another. They explained that the heart has many parts to it. This was the part I had hidden away when I was receiving threat and torture for being who I am and knowing what I know. I decided to lock it away and make it difficult for me to find so that I would not endure such pain again or place myself in harm's way. The enchanted box that was designed to keep me forever seeking was to keep working until such time came when it would be safe for me to uncover my magical powers once again. Now was that time.

The Beings of the Light placed my heart within me. As they did, it changed from a fleshy red color to one that was golden. I heard the phrase "a heart of gold." What I felt at that moment is difficult to describe. It was not happiness, although I was happy. It was more like a knowing or a calm wisdom that came back to me. I had a greater sense of myself.

I am very grateful to have been given the wisdom of how to retrieve the pieces of my heart that have been hidden or given away. I hope my experiences have inspired you to go looking for your missing or hidden heart pieces and bring them home where they belong.

Applying the Wisdom

If you are someone who has a back-up plan, worries about being abandoned, or left without someone to love you, please do the inner child exercises I described previously. They will help.

If you have someone from your past who keeps entering your thoughts, have a heart-to-heart talk with them, and ask Archangel Michael to assist in the retrieval of any heart and soul fragments that need to be returned to you. Archangel Michael is greatly skilled in this work and will make the transfer easy and gentle. Then check to see if you are holding onto any heart or soul fragments of others that need to be returned. You may be surprised at how many you are carrying. When it is no longer beneficial to be carrying these fragments, they can feel like a burden or a responsibility that weighs upon your shoulders. If the person you are carrying them for is not ready to receive them back, ask that the archangels or The Beings of the Light carry them instead. They will gladly take this on for you and they certainly can be trusted to love, nurture, and honor anything that comes into their care.

Imagine a heart and soul fragment exchange if someone has broken your heart, if you love someone or something but can't set them free, or if you have moved to a new house and your heart is still in the old one. One thing I have learned from this process is that your heart needs to travel with you at all times.

Again, do all this work using your imagination and allowing your intuition to provide you with the imagery necessary. Follow it wherever it takes you. It is an easy process and only requires a willingness to truly notice what is there.

CHAPTER 18

✷

The Haunting, The Hanging, and The Dungeon

"I shut my eyes in order to see." – Paul Gaugin

When I regained the aspect of my heart I needed in order to gain the remaining ideas to share in this book, I had a feeling I was going to receive my next chapter that night.

Before I went to sleep, I felt compelled to read a few chapters out of a neglected book that was sitting on my nightstand. The book was Colette Baron Reid's *Remembering the Future* in which she tells the story of her journey to becoming a renowned intuitive. It was no accident I had held off reading further in this book until now. Turns out the information I read that night was exactly what I needed to help me write my next chapter.

Colette described a time when she was struggling with the idea of who she thought she wanted to be and accepting the truth of who she really was. She told the story of hearing guidance that told her to pay attention to the true inner vision she was receiving from her intuition and less attention to the outer vision her mind wanted to create for herself. I understood immediately that the same message was for me. I had been feeling anxiety over writing this book, wondering what would become of it, hoping that it would be a success. My outer vision included me becoming a published author, well known as a spiritual teacher, and having this book leap me forward in my career. The anxiety should have been a clue that I was ignoring the true inner vision. I was already coming to realize that my writing about what was happening to me on this journey was bringing up issues that needed to be healed. Perhaps this book was only to serve to help me. I didn't want it to be. I wanted it to be something that others might resonate with, to see their story in mine, and use my journey as a means to help them along their way. I wasn't sure, but I knew it was time to find out the truth. What happened next was one of the most profound inner journeys I have ever been taken on.

I closed my eyes and asked to be shown the true inner vision regarding this book. Immediately, I saw myself running on a dirt road. I came up to a wooden fence that housed a yard on which several buildings stood. There was a barn, a blacksmith's shop, and a house. I knew that I was watching myself enter into a place I had been before. It was the place where I once lived long ago in another lifetime.

What was odd about this vision was that it was completely in black and white, like an old western movie. It had a western feel to it too. The buildings were all empty. It was like a ghost town.

I opened the gate to the property and began walking around. This place did not seem safe, yet I knew I was in no danger. There really was no one else there but me. I came upon the house that was on the property. It was a modest, square, two-story home. I knew I had a room in this house. It was located upstairs and I knew it still contained some of my precious things.

I could sense that the house was haunted. I didn't dare enter it. Why was I here? I had asked for the true inner vision regarding this book. Immediately, I got the message that I was haunted by my past. Until I could free myself from this place, I could not see the rest of my true vision. I guess you could say it was a ghost town, containing my very own ghosts.

I remembered I had told myself I would never step foot in that house again. I had no plans to break my promise. This house and whatever was in it, I was going to leave behind. I asked if there was anything of value and importance to me that still remained in the house that it finds its way to me. Just as I was about to walk away, three objects from my room summoned my attention. I didn't need to go into the house to get them. They appeared before me and fell into my hands.

The first item was a leather-bound journal that had a feather pen attached to it. This represented my freedom to write as I wished. The journal was a place where I could write my true feelings and ideas down without fear of persecution, judgment, or blame. I knew this was significant because in this life, I had often tried to keep journals and diaries, but would never write what I was truly feeling in them. I was too afraid someone might find it, read it, and then use it against me. This was especially true when I was younger, in my teens and twenties.

The second item was a magic wand that had a beautiful, glowing quartz crystal at the end of it. This represented my ability to perform magic and I knew somewhere deep within me that I had used this wand in very magical and mystical ways before. Memories of being a sorceress were being stirred within me. I saw visions of me being like Merlin, and knowledgeable in alchemy. By receiving this wand, I was reclaiming my right to perform magic.

The third and final item was a crystal ball that represented my clairvoyance. I needed it in order to see the rest of my true inner vision. I thanked all the items for making their way back to me and placed them in a satchel I was carrying.

I knew it was time to leave this place for good. What this vision was telling me was that it was not a place where I once lived. It was the place where I lived, day to day, haunted by the past, afraid of being who I was and how powerful I could become. I asked if there was anything else I needed to learn from this place. I was told "No." An angel appeared and showed me a portal that would take me to the next leg of my true inner vision.

As I stepped through the portal, I felt like I was back where I started. I was in the same ghost town, but this time there was a path that led out to a field. I followed the path and came to a hanging platform. The platform stood about 3 feet off the ground with struts secured above high enough to adequately carry a noose. I knew instinctively I had been hanged there.

I sat on the platform remembering everything. I remembered the lynch mob laughing and cheering as I was brought onto the platform. I remembered my hands being tied behind my back and a large man escorting me to stand on a small box. The man had a black hood over his face so that I couldn't see it. I remembered the noose going around my neck and the box being kicked out from underneath me. Tears streamed down my face as I remembered.

I stood up on the platform and looked at the place where I remembered myself hanging. As I remembered, I saw myself hanging there. I cut myself down and laid myself gently on the platform. I removed the noose and untied my hands. I held myself in my arms and told me that I loved me. I said I forgave myself for this happening. I told myself that I had done nothing wrong and that I was ok. I looked out and could see the lynch mob. I forgave them too. As I forgave them, they disappeared. I saw the man who put the noose around my neck and I forgave him. He, then too, disappeared. I continued to hold my hanged self in my arms and feeling so much love. I watched as my hanged self died. My spirit floated up out of the body that lay in my arms and smiled at me. She was the most beautiful golden and yellow light. She told me that she was completely at peace and this pain could now forever be put to rest. Then she travelled upwards to heaven while sparkly light sprinkles rained upon me.

I buried my hanged self and marked the grave with a heart shaped stone. I placed flowers atop the grave, and honored the body that housed the beautiful spirit I had just seen ascend into heaven. I treated myself with respect, the respect that I had been searching for my entire life.

Before I left this place, I dismantled the hanging platform and piled it into a heap of wood. I took out my magic wand that I now carried with me, and with my intent, started the entire heap on fire where it, the noose, the rope which tied my hands, and the trauma burned completely away never to harm me or another ever again.

When I looked behind me, the ghost town was no longer there. It had vanished with the rest of the memories. I had wiped the slate clean.

An angel appeared once again and told me it was time to enter into the next leg of this journey to my true inner vision. As I stepped into a light portal I was transported this time into a dark, dank dungeon. Water dripped from the black walls and there was the stench of death in the air.

I could tell I was in a holding cell. There were iron bars locking me in on one side. Everywhere else was rock. At the back of the cell, I noticed a very old man shackled at his hands, feet, and neck to the wall. He was so emaciated that there wasn't much left of him except skin and bones. I went to him, pulled out my magic wand, and broke the shackles free. I carefully picked him up into my arms. He felt like he weighed no more than a small child, even though he was a grown man. A soft bed of white light appeared and I gently placed him on it. I held his hand and stroked his hair telling him that I loved him and that he had done nothing wrong. I told him that he was a beautiful light and not to believe anything else despite what he had been through or been told. I told him I was going to get him out of this place, that he didn't need to stay here any longer. I opened the iron bar doors with my magic wand and gently guided him on his bed of light out of the cell. We continued on through a maze of hallways through this dungeon, but I instinctively knew the way out. I brought the man to the surface. His weak eyes adjusted to the light gradually. He smiled the most beautiful toothless smile and tears ran down my eyes. I very much loved this man. I told him, "Grandpa, you're free now. You can go now. You needn't suffer any longer. The light is waiting for you."

I watched his spirit ascend and free itself from the suffering it had endured for lifetimes. I watched him dance his way to heaven, rejoicing and laughing the entire way.

Something profound happened during this leg of the journey. I knew that the man I had freed was my grandfather – my dad's dad. I never met him in this life. He died before I was born. From what I understand he was a strict man and father. From this meeting, I understood why he was the way he was. He was trying to protect his family from the suffering he had endured and was enduring, as a tortured man shackled and left to die of starvation in a dungeon. The fear of the consequences of one of his loved ones stepping out of line with the church or any authority would have been so great that he felt compelled to rule with an iron fist. It is no wonder he was the way he was.

I also knew that in freeing him, I had freed myself and any other family member caught in the ancestral karma of this circumstance. I often had felt like my hands were tied and my feet were shackled without really knowing why. I, too, carried great fear of being banished to the dungeon for making a mistake or breaking from the status quo. I understood that in order for me to be able to move forward on my journey, I needed to free him and me of this ancestral karma. I must admit, I certainly felt freer.

My guiding angel appeared once more to take me to the next leg of this journey. The angel motioned me to enter the next light portal. I did so, eager to see what was going to be on the other side.

This time I was transported into a crystal cave. Inside was a person who was dressed in a cape, much like you would expect a magician to be dressed. I could tell this person was hiding something. He seemed very nervous, almost frantic. I recognized that this man was an aspect of myself.

Because of his magical powers, he recognized immediately that he was not alone in his cave. He shouted, "Who's there?" again using his body to hide what he was protecting behind him. I told him that it was I. I explained that I was he, and that I had come from the future in a quest to find my true inner vision. He calmed down immediately and said he had something to show me.

He brought into view what he had been hiding. It was a rectangular box that had been converted into a makeshift crib. Inside was a two-headed baby, who was badly disfigured and fussing. At first, I had trouble putting these pieces together. I knew the baby partly represented my book and partly something else. Did it mean that this book was going to turn out badly? I knew that wasn't the right answer the moment I asked.

I turned to the man and looked into his eyes. Deep sadness filled them. It was the same sadness I recognized in myself. It was the sadness I felt about not being able to be who I truly was. Writing this book was certainly going to expose all that. That's when it clicked. I knew what it all meant.

I was carrying the belief that who I truly was inside was a freak. Like the two-headed disfigured baby, if I exposed who I truly was through this book, I feared I would be viewed as a freak that people would mock and laugh at. I said the baby partly represented my book. In a way, the book was my baby. I was its mother, creating it and hoping to give birth to it and proudly show it to the world. The other part the baby represented was me and who I truly was. I was different. I was not like the status quo. To truly be who I am, I knew I couldn't hide that any longer. I had to show the world my freakiness.

I picked the two-headed baby up into my arms and held it to my heart. The baby stopped fussing and began cooing. I sent it all the love I had within me and told it telepathically that I knew it was perfect. I told the baby I accepted it for who it was, and loved it unconditionally. As I did this, the baby began to transform in my arms. When I looked down, the baby had changed into a glowing, valentine-shaped heart. It was no longer freakishly disfigured. It turned into a symbol of love. I showed my other self, the man who I first noticed when I entered the cave, the heart and tears welled up in his eyes. The sadness that was held in those eyes was now washed away with joy and elation. A sense of relief flooded the both of us. We were now free to be us!

The man took the heart in his hands and gently folded it. He took the journal that had appeared to me at the haunted house, opened it, and placed the heart inside. He told me telepathically, "This is your book. It is safe to share your heart with the world now." He handed the journal back to me, smiled a wonderful, mischievous smile like the Cheshire Cat, and with a wave of his cape, vanished into thin air. I knew he had been freed, too. I wished him well.

The guiding angel, who had been with me on this entire journey, appeared once again. "Are you ready to see your true inner vision?" I nodded. The angel motioned me to enter the final light portal and leg of this journey. Before I did, I looked back at the crystal cave and thanked it for keeping me safe while I needed the protection.

The portal transported me somewhere up in the sky. It was how I might have imagined heaven when I was a little girl. I was standing on clouds and I could hear beautiful, angelic music in the background. I was motioned to sit on a stool at a table. On the table was a box with two drawers. I was told the top drawer contained the outcome if I continue to control the process of what this book is to be and the bottom drawer contained the outcome of the true inner vision, of what could happen if I just allow the book to be what it is meant to be.

I opened the top drawer. It reminded me of a junk drawer, one of those drawers everyone has where you put all the junk in you don't have any place else for. It looked disorganized and messy. I didn't want this. I closed this drawer and opened the other one.

This drawer slid out easily. Inside was pure light. I couldn't see any specific outcome, but I could feel it. I could feel a lightness, a happiness, and a freedom I don't think I have ever felt before. I didn't know how this was going to play out in my everyday life. I didn't know what this outcome was going to look like. But if it felt like this, I knew it would be good. This is what I wanted.

I asked to be shown some of what this meant. I saw my husband and children standing by my side beaming. They were proud of me. They also were very excited. This let me know that while this book would be beneficial for me, it would also be beneficial for my family.

I tried to ascertain whether my book would sell a lot of copies or if it would be well received, but was unable to get the answers. I was told that was part of what my mind wanted to envision, not part of the true vision. I was also told that I wasn't actually ready to accept everything that may come out of this, but to trust the feelings I found in the second drawer. This is why I had to write this book, not to sell a million copies, not to gain the title of published author, but instead to feel that feeling of lightness and freedom of who I am.

Applying the Wisdom

Sit quietly with your eyes closed and ask to be shown the true inner vision of your life or some part of it. Allow your imagination to show you whatever it is you need to see and let it take you on a journey. Do not be disappointed if you don't get the answer right away. Like me, you may need to clear away some past haunts before you can get to where you want to be.

My experience that I describe above is an excellent example of a combination of past life memory and magical, multidimensional metaphor. The symbolism laid within this experience is great and varied and also illustrates the importance of trusting the information you receive. I, in no way, can verify through proof that the man in the dungeon was my grandfather. I just know it was him. Trust what you know even if you can't explain how or why you know it. Your intuition is never wrong. If it feels right, it is. If it feels wrong, it is.

The Three Gifts of the Magi

The Beings of the Light told me that the experience of receiving the three items from the house was similar to receiving the three gifts of the Magi. If you would like to receive your forgotten gifts, follow these steps.

Sit quietly with your eyes closed and ask to receive the gifts that you require to continue on your path of light. Allow each gift to show itself to you. Do not try to make the gifts what you want, but instead allow them to be what you need. If you receive a gift or a symbol that you do not understand, ask to be told what it means. Then listen and watch for the answer. If you are unable to ascertain a meaning, it is likely because you are not ready or willing to know. Trust you will find out when the time is right.

Have fun with these exercises. Finding a true inner vision and your inner gifts should be exciting and enjoyable. The gifts will help you fulfill your true inner vision. Know that whatever the true inner vision is, it has to be good. The light never delivers darkness.

CHAPTER 19

Making Friends with the Ego

"You'll never feel alone if you like the person you are alone with." – Dr. Wayne Dyer

My 8-year-old daughter was having difficulties in her relationship with her best friend at school. She was upset because her best friend had decided to play with other girls and exclude her. This came from a falling out over some disagreement on the playground at recess.

It's tough as a mother to see your children hurting. I could tell my daughter was both mad at her friend and feeling insecure about her worth. I knew if she was going to successfully make it through this, she had to let go of any blame she was directing at her friend and find that place of confidence and love inside of her to know she would be ok no matter what the outcome of this became. But how?

Every night before our children go to sleep, my husband and I alternate lying down and saying good night with each of our daughters. This gives us a little one-on-one time with them that we may not get at any other time in the day. My youngest daughter calls it "having a little snuggle." It was my night to have a little snuggle with my eldest girl.

I asked The Beings of the Light to assist me in guiding her in the best way to resolve her issue with her friend. They immediately showed me what to do.

I asked my daughter to close her eyes and imagine her inner best friend. This isn't her actual best friend in real life, but the one that lives inside her. When she saw her, I asked her to connect to that friend and feel the love and support she had for her. I asked her to feel how much this inner best friend loved her. She did. Then, I asked her to imagine herself merging with her inner best friend so that her best friend became her and she became her best friend. In this way, she becomes her own best friend.

I could tell immediately that she felt more confident and at ease with the situation. Often, we expect others to provide us with love and happiness. We expect others to give us friendship, when all the while we have it within ourselves. When we acknowledge the presence of friendship within, we will experience the presence of friendship without. The next day my daughter came home from school saying that things were back to normal with her best friend and that they played all day together. This is the magic of working in the 5th dimension. It immediately changes what's going on in the 3rd.

My daughter fell asleep quickly that night, and as I lay myself down to sleep, The Beings of the Light asked me to do the same exercise. One thing I immediately noticed when I acknowledged that I am my own best friend is that I was not alone. I had an inner companion who was always with me, cheering me on and believing in me.

The Beings of the Light then told me that this exercise could be used to connect with any aspect of myself. We carry all aspects of any relationship inside ourselves. By using this technique, we can improve our relationships with others by acknowledging that there is a similar, very loving relationship within.

They asked me to call forth my divine inner wife – the aspect of me that was a wife. I could tell immediately that I had not been connecting with her. As I realized how much love was available for me as a wife, I felt more confident and more lovingly connected to my husband. I want to make clear that this has nothing to do with my husband, who is a kind, wonderful man. This disconnection has to do with my own insecurities of not measuring up. As I reconnected with my divine inner wife, those insecurities faded into nothingness.

Next, they asked me to connect with my divine inner husband. We have aspects of all the people in our lives within and the inner husband is no exception. When I imagined him, I noticed how much pressure I put on him and how much I expected of him. I wasn't allowing him to love me. I was too busy finding fault with him. When I relaxed and noticed just how much he adored me, I allowed him to come closer and hug me. He and my divine inner wife joined together in a union of love, a wedding without vows. It was beautiful. I felt amazing.

Since I felt I was getting the hang of this, I asked to connect with the aspect of myself that was a divine published author. Getting this book published was still a fear for me, and I knew I had to connect with the author within in order to experience being an author in my outer world. At first, she wasn't present at all, but I knew she was in me somewhere. I asked to make herself known. When I finally was able to imagine her, I was very detached from her. She seemed far away to me. I asked her to come closer and I invited her to become part of me. This wasn't easy, because I could tell I was afraid to allow her to become part of my experience.

As my inner author came closer, I could tell that she was insecure. I called forth my inner best friend and together, as one, we encouraged the inner author to be all she could be. We gave her confidence. As soon as I believed she could be a great inner author, she became one. I wasn't able to do this without the help of my inner best friend. I then allowed the inner author to merge with me so that I became her and she became me. For the first time I felt like this was really happening. I was going to become what I had been hoping for. I understood immediately that this explained the notion that in order to create it, you had to believe it could actually happen. I was no longer afraid that it wouldn't happen. More importantly, I was no longer afraid that it would.

This was becoming fun and I wanted to do more. The Beings of the Light suggested I call forth my inner mother. As I did, I could feel her love for me. I could feel myself being cradled in loving arms. I could feel her believing in me. (Note: This may not be your initial experience. If it's not, stick with your inner mother until you accept her love for you. You are the inner mother, just as you are the inner wife or husband and the inner best friend. When you love yourself, you will feel the love of the inner mother.)

Mother energy represents the relationships in our life. When we are connected to our inner mother, we will be nurturing, loving, compassionate, and understanding in our relationships with others.

Next, I was asked to call forth my inner father. I didn't feel an immediate love from my inner father like I did with my inner mother. Instead, I felt scared that I wasn't enough. I felt that I hadn't done enough to earn my inner father's approval. Again, this had nothing to do with my actual father, but had everything to do with my inner thoughts of myself as a daughter. These feelings highlighted the areas where I felt like a failure or that I couldn't measure up to some invisible high standard I had created in my mind. When I allowed my inner father to love me and approve of me, I felt calmer and more complete. When I allowed him to pat me on the back and encourage me, I felt capable. When I allowed my inner father to be proud of me, I felt accepted and validated.

Father energy represents our ability to do and create in the world. It is connected to career and the way we provide for ourselves and others. In this way, father energy represents our self-worth and the ability to see ourselves as worthy and deserving of wonderful things. When we are connected to our inner father in love, we will feel like we are enough. We no longer will feel like we have to do more to be more. Instead, we will feel like we can just be.

My night was spent meeting more aspects of myself. I called forth my inner goddess. She encouraged me to connect to my inner sexuality. This is not easy for me to mention, because I grew up in a household where sex was rarely mentioned. If it was, it was in the context of "don't do it until you're married and once you do it, don't talk about it." If it makes you uncomfortable reading this, perhaps you have what I had – an unhealthy view of your own sexuality.

I had kept my sexuality so private that when I tried to call it forth, I could tell it was hiding. I was afraid to let her out, because someone else might notice her! I was afraid of being labeled a slut and a whore. It was becoming clearer and clearer to me that I did have an unhealthy view of my sexuality, for I was neither a slut nor a whore. My inner best friend encouraged my sexuality to come out telling it that it was beautiful and feminine – two things that I rarely felt. I could tell I had hidden the aspects of my beauty and femininity away to protect them from harsh judgments of others. I was keeping them safe.

As the beautiful, feminine inner sexuality emerged, it became clear to me that she didn't need protecting. She carried more power and strength with her than I ever imagined. I used to think femininity and beauty somehow made me weak or were weak and thus, needed protecting. The truth was they were part of my inner strength, and it was time to acknowledge and unleash their power.

Before I truly could accept and connect with my sexuality, I had to release all the beliefs that thousands of years of patriarchy and societal pressures of what it meant to be a good woman had placed upon me. It was time to shed the old ideas and distorted view of the sacred feminine. Being a woman meant having the power of attraction and command. It meant being able to stand in one's beauty and power and not apologize for it. I could see why others wanted to beat this power down. It can be intimidating. At closer look, however, there is a warmth and sacredness to it. There is the ability to create life and the ability to empower others to see the beauty and power within themselves. It is something to be revered and acknowledged, not hidden away.

The beauty of the feminine energy is that it resides in us all regardless of gender. We have both feminine and masculine energies within. When a man honors the feminine energy within, he becomes stronger and more powerful, not emasculated, as he may fear. The divine feminine energy is present to allow the divine masculine to adore and honor her. This is what makes a man a man. The purpose of the divine feminine is to allow herself to be adored and honored. When she does, she owns her innate powers of attraction and command and allows the divine masculine to burst with pride and love for her. He will do anything in her name. When she denies him that right, he feels small, insignificant, and resentful.

I could see areas where I was not allowing myself to be honored and adored. It was time for this to stop. The easiest way was for me to connect with the divine feminine within and she was certainly tied into my sexuality. It's the same for us all. I allowed the divine masculine part of me to honor and adore this part of me. As I allowed this to happen, I could feel the feminine, sexual part of me grow into a beautiful, beaming light. As I let that light grow, I could tell it had to do with much more than sexuality. It primarily had to do with creativity and our ability to express ourselves in love. It had to do with passion, not only sexual passion, but passion for life and passion for expressing ourselves creatively from the depths of our soul. In essence, it is the expression of our truth, of who we truly are, which is unique to every person. It's interesting that sexuality is an area where we, as humanity, have tried to conform and restrain. No wonder it hasn't worked. Conformity and restraint are the antithesis to this part of us, which is expansive, creative, and needs freedom to grow.

It is the time for the sacred feminine to come out of hiding and allow itself to be honored and adored once more. This is not to say that we will shift from a patriarchy to a matriarchy. Instead, it is more of a coming into balance with the masculine and the feminine, working together, instead of against each other, as a unified team.

Whether you are a woman or a man, it is important to bring your masculine and feminine energies into balance. Use this technique to help you. Some of you will be like me – one needing to honor the sacred feminine within. Others will find that you honor the sacred feminine but are afraid of the divine masculine's power. Instead of fearing your divine masculine power, love it. Allow it to honor and adore you and it will come back into balance and grow within you through love. Feel the gratitude for its presence to provide for you. When you allow the divine masculine to do its job of caring for you, you help it to be a man. When it cares for you and loves you for who you are, the divine masculine helps you to be a woman. This creates a human in perfect, loving balance.

I encourage you to use this technique with as many aspects of yourself as you can imagine. If you manage to make the love connection with the aspect you are working with, the effects of this exercise are immediate and very healing to what has been damaged within. Understand that if you find your inner mother isn't loving you, it's not her doing. It's you not allowing her to love you. If your inner father isn't approving of you, it has nothing to do with him. It's you not allowing your inner father to approve of you. You have to allow them to love you. It's only you and your ego holding yourself from what you desire, no one else.

I Am Not My Feelings

I was recently watching an interview with Lady Gaga where she told a story of how she was once thrown in the trash by bullies as a young girl. This stuck with her and you could tell in the interview it still hurt, even though she was able to rise above. It made me think of times in my life when I felt I was treated like trash. Like Lady Gaga, I still felt the pain of those experiences. The Beings of the Light spoke to me in the kindest way asking, "When those boys threw Lady Gaga in the trash, did that make her trash?" I thought about their question carefully. "No, it didn't make her trash. It made her feel like trash."

"Exactly," said The Beings of the Light. "You know her to be quite precious. You know she has an important light to shine in the world, just as everyone does. If she allowed herself to become her feelings, she would not have rose above, picked herself out of the trash, and recognized the precious treasure that she is within. You are not your feelings. You are a Light Being. They (the bullies) are not their feelings of hate and anger. They are Light Beings. It takes a light to shine in order for those who are not shining to realize they have a light within too. This is why love heals. Love is light, and when it shines it can heal. Love is not so much a feeling or an emotion as it is who you are."

I thought about what they said. "I am not my feelings. I am love." I knew it was very difficult to separate ourselves from our feelings. The Beings of the Light spoke again, "Your feelings are nothing more than a representation of your thoughts. When you think a thought over and over again, so much so that you believe it, that thought will produce a feeling. Let's say you feel that you are unlovable. That feeling was produced by a combination of many thoughts that said you are unlovable. Those thoughts were formed by thinking that the unloving acts of others somehow defined who you are.

Remember that you are not your feelings. Just because you feel unlovable, it does not mean you are unlovable. It only means you think you are. What you are and what you think you are, is not the same thing. It may feel like the same thing because you think you are your feelings. But what you feel and what you are is not the same thing. It is time to write this as a new belief into your programming."

"You can do that? How?" I asked.

"Believe," they said to me. "I sat in silence trying to get a feel for what was happening to me. I felt like things were different, but couldn't quite place my finger on exactly what had changed. I intuitively got the image of a computer program with its many ones and zeros flashing and changing before me. I could feel the rewriting of my programming occurring deep within my chest. I began to breathe deeply. The pressure I often felt in the center of my chest was morphing. I could hear the words, "I am not my feelings. I am not my thoughts. I am love." quite strongly in my body. I could sense the fight of my ego wanting to hang onto its existence. I observed as my ego was being shown that it was love too. My ego was also being reprogrammed. It was learning that it didn't need rules in order to exist. It was learning that it too could be just as it was – a piece of God's creation. My ego said it didn't know how to judge me if it couldn't make rules to decide what was right and wrong. It was told it no longer needed to judge me. It was told it could just accept me for who I am and let me be. My ego was showered in love. "You are not a hateful thing. You are love." I could feel the ego fight against the words. I could see the ego trying to get me to believe I was awful by showing me hurtful things of the past. All I could think of was that I was love and it was loved for showing me. Then the ego just stopped fighting. The reprogramming continued for some time. As it did, I increasingly felt calmer and more at ease.

The ego popped up one more time and said, "I don't know how to be love. What do I do?" The reprogramming had taken its rules away and it felt lost. It didn't know how to be. It needed a job. I asked that it help me fulfill my soul purpose and heart's desires by keeping me connected to the divine mind. Knowing that this was going to be a much easier job than it had previously, ego asked me in the sweetest childlike voice if it could play. I asked how it wanted to play. It replied, "I want to make you laugh more." I agreed and immediately began laughing out loud. I felt that ego had become a friend in me instead of my enemy.

Love is the essence of who we are. Our thoughts and feelings are the essence of our human experience, but are not who we are. If we are to create an experience of who we are as a human, then we must always remember when an unpleasant feeling shows itself, to say, "This is not who I am. I am love." In recognizing that we are love, we will come to believe it and feel it.

Since the reprogramming, I have been aware of subtle changes. I am not as judgmental of myself or others, and feel more calm inside. I find myself forgiving those who judge me and accepting them for their perspective, all the while understanding that their thoughts have no reflection on me. It seems I am beginning to truly separate who I am from what I feel.

Applying the Wisdom
Connecting with Your Inner Aspects

Sit quietly with your eyes closed. Ask whatever aspect of yourself you wish to connect with to make itself known to you. Pay attention to whatever comes to your imagination. Get a sense of where it is. Sometimes it will be right in front of your face and sometimes it will be hiding. If it isn't totally loving and accepting of you it is because you are not totally loving and accepting of it. Find the strength, ability, and perfection of this aspect of yourself. Notice how it responds, fills with light, and grows as you do. Once the aspect of yourself is totally in support of you and you feel its unconditional love for you, allow its image to merge with you so that the two of you become one.

If you are calling forth a feminine aspect of you make sure you call forth the masculine counterpart as well, and vice-versa. You want to balance the masculine and feminine energies within.

Some other very beneficial aspects that you can call forth using this technique are the inner sister/brother, inner grandmother/grandfather, inner boss/employee, inner boyfriend/girlfriend, inner aunt/uncle, or inner niece/nephew. You can also call forth different characteristics of the self like your inner confidence/insecurity, inner bully/victim, inner wealth/poverty, and so on. The reason why you would want to call forth negative aspects of the self such as the inner bully and victim is because when you love and accept all aspects of yourself, those aspects will become loving and accepting of you.

You may find there is an aspect of yourself that needs to be connected with often until the connection becomes habit. For me, it is the frequent connection with my inner father that seems to have the most beneficial impact for me. Find out who it is for you. First and foremost however, always be connected to your inner best friend. S/He will provide you with the strength and encouragement to connect with the others and remind you that you are never alone in the process.

Reprogramming Beliefs

Ask The Beings of the Light for a rewrite of your programming to suit your highest good and the highest good of all involved. Sit in awareness and observe any thoughts or feelings that arise as the process is in progress. You will instinctively know when it is complete. Give yourself some time to experience this process – perhaps a half an hour to an hour where you will not be interrupted. Allow the process to unfold. Avoid trying to make it something that it is not or to control the process. You do not know the best way to rewrite your programming. If you did, you would have done it by now. Allow the Light to do its work and provide you with what it is you need.

CHAPTER 20

A Path of Your Own Making

"Understand that the right to choose your own path is a sacred privilege. Use it. Dwell in possibility." – Oprah Winfrey

The Beings of the Light have spent a great deal of time with me exploring my path and teaching me how I can assist others in creating an easier, more enjoyable, light-filled path of their own. They say that the path that we visualize in relation to any given situation will provide all the answers as to why things are they way they are. Altering the path by using one's imagination is an easy, yet effective way to create change. The Beings of the Light call the path the ultimate magical multidimensional metaphor.

When I work with a client, I will often be guided to ask them to imagine the path they are walking. Their description of this path gives immediate clues as to what is going on in their world, what they are creating, and how it can easily be changed to better suit their needs.

You can tell a lot about a person's journey just by finding out what material they are walking on. Is it gravel, concrete, brick, asphalt, dirt, grass, or something entirely different? Ideally, you want to be walking on something that is pleasurable on the bare feet. A gravel path is a rocky path and hurts the feet when walked upon. If I come across a person whose path is made of gravel, I ask them to change it to something softer and smoother, something that has a nice feel under foot and has some give to it. This change alone can make a person's life easier and more pleasurable.

One night, I asked my 6-year-old daughter to imagine her path. When I asked her to describe what it was like, she replied, "Bouncy." This description fit perfectly because she absolutely bounces through life just as a six year old should. At this point, I had already done considerable work on my path, but never considered the actual material on which I was walking. My path was made of concrete. I never realized how this could be a problem, until now. My daughter let me know with one word that a path does not need to be rigid and inflexible. It was no wonder that I have had issues with my knees. I was walking on concrete all the time! My path didn't have any give in it. This is also kind of how I viewed life at the time – hard and unforgiving. I also have been known to be quite headstrong and stubborn, not very flexible in my opinions. The concrete was a metaphor for all these things. That night, I changed my path to add more bounce into it. When I did, it immediately felt like life was more forgiving, carefree, and whimsical. I also felt like I could effortlessly leap forward and have fun in the process.

A question that The Beings of the Light taught me to ask when working with my path was, "Show me how my path could even be better than it is now." After I changed my path from concrete to something with a little more bounce in it, I asked "Show me how I can make it even better than this." When I did, I saw my path transform into a rainbow of colors. Not only was my path bouncy, but it was now colorful and really beautiful. I liked that.

Check if you are able to easily move forward on your path. Are you actually standing on your path or viewing it from a distance? Are there any obstructions or obstacles in your way? Is it safe to move forward? If your path is blocked, you must find your way around, through, or over the obstacle. Make this as easy as possible.

As I mentioned previously, I have an uncle who was diagnosed with prostate cancer. He told me that he viewed the cancer as a big rock in the middle of his path that he just has to get around so that he can continue on his journey. We began working with this imagery. His subconscious mind was already providing him with the metaphor of what cancer meant to him. When I asked him how big the rock was, he said it was like a big boulder, too high to climb and too large to just walk around. We needed to figure out a way to either remove the rock or leave it behind him. Chipping away at the rock seemed like a lot of effort for little gain. Trying to go around felt like he could get lost and lose his way. Staying where he was felt like a death sentence. The Beings of the Light showed me that he was to float above it so that he could view the situation from a higher perspective. To get there he could simply become lighter than air and float, or he could take an elevator that they installed to take him to the top of it. He liked the imagery of floating, used it, and immediately felt more in control of the situation. He also felt like he could see his way past the boulder and it was comforting to know there was life on the other side.

A few weeks later, my uncle sent me an email stating that, in meditation, he was now sitting on top of the boulder in his path and he was being shown a number of different directions he could take once he climbed down onto the other side. He just needed to decide which new path to walk.

That night I was given a message that I was to relay to my uncle. I was told that he was to no longer view the rock on his path as a large boulder, but instead as a pebble. To do this he could either make himself so large that the boulder appeared to him as a pebble, or he could shrink the rock to the size of a small stone and see the mountain for what it really was - a molehill. The Beings of the Light showed me that his subconscious mind was viewing the cancer as a big, hard, strong, powerful rock when in truth, it was nothing more than a small stone in his shoe causing irritation. They told me that this is how society views cancer and that making it big, strong, and scary is just the fear it needs to feed on to survive. When you remove the fear and see it as nothing more than a pebble in your shoe, it loses all power. Fear always makes things appear larger and scarier than they really are.

People fear that cancer can take their life. A big rock is sure enough to squash you, cut off your air supply, or block your life from moving forward. These are powerful metaphors. Most people want to fight cancer. They even use those words, "I'm going to fight it." Needing to fight means you have an opponent and to fight means you put yourself in danger. You get hurt in a fight. It is not the best course of action. If you view cancer as an attacker, you leave no choice but to fight. If you don't, you get beat up. But if you view cancer as a pebble that you picked up walking on your gravelly path, you don't have to fight and you don't have to see it as a threat. It becomes merely something that has to be dealt with. You have to stop in your tracks, sit down, and shake the stones out of your shoes. That's what cancer does. It stops people in their tracks. They just forget to think that maybe it's nothing more than a pebble – a minor irritation that needs addressing. Instead, they do as many before them have done. They become afraid and decide they are under attack. Then they fight what is often seen as a losing battle. But it doesn't have to be that way. What if being stopped in your tracks is the break that you need to gain some perspective? Perhaps what is needed is to stop so that you can see there are other options available to you and allow you to move in a direction better suited to fulfilling your heart's desires. In this way, cancer now becomes a blessing. That is, if you are willing to allow yourself to view it that way.

My uncle had mentioned that he was looking at a variety of new paths to take while he sat upon his rock. The other message I received for him was to make sure one of those paths included the option to carry a clean bill of health and to be able to live life with joy moving forward. If that path was not one of the options, then to ask where that option exists. He will be shown. Once shown, then it is up to him to decide to step onto that path.

This leads me to the next point about altering your path. Not only can you change what is currently on your path, you can also change the path altogether. If the path you are on is leading nowhere or is leaving you feeling lost and frustrated, simply ask your higher guidance to show you the path that would be most beneficial for you to walk right now. Pay attention to what you are being shown. Sometimes a door will appear that you will have to open and walk through. Sometimes, your path will come to a fork in the road and you will need to choose to change direction. Sometimes the path will be above you, meaning you will need to allow yourself to rise above your circumstances and walk the higher road. If it's above you, float up and put yourself on it. If you can't seem to get yourself to where you want to be, it is because you are not allowing yourself to go there. Ask for any ties that are keeping you on the less beneficial path to be cut and any commitments to be fulfilled in the name of the light so that you are free to change paths, then go. This can happen in a matter of seconds. It doesn't need to take a long time. Remember, the imagination is the gateway to the 5th dimension where you transcend time and space.

Notice where your path is leading you and the journey you will have to make to get there. What is in the distance? This represents your future. Is your path taking you to something wanted? If not, ask for the best road that will lead you to your heart's desires. Often, people will discover it is dark in the distance and that they cannot see what lies ahead. Again, you could shine light on it, have the sun come out, or open your third eye by imagining an eye in the center of the forehead opening and really take a look at what is there.

It is also important to get a feel for where you are headed. Does it feel good? Does it feel like a trap? Use your imagination to shift things accordingly. Generally, if something is light or glowing with light, then that is a key to your higher road. Light represents love. Dark represents fear. Choose the light over dark in every instance.

How long is the journey to what you want? If it's a long uphill climb, then shorten and flatten the path. As I was writing this book, I was viewing my path as a deep descent down a hill, followed by a long uphill climb to get to a beautiful white castle. I knew the castle represented my dreams come true. I didn't like the long, arduous journey there. I asked my higher guidance to help me find an easier way. Immediately, the deep valley that separated me from my castle was filled in with white light and a rainbow bridge appeared with a knight in shining armor there to escort me safely across. Just as I was imagining this, I was resting my feet on top of my coffee table where I had a stick of incense burning. I burned the bottom of my foot on the incense. I knew this was a sign. I said to myself, "I will not allow myself to be burned in this process." Just then, I realized I was feeling like I had to follow some other authority's wishes, like I had to go down the hard path in order to be rewarded with my prize. Since the authority felt like a boss, I said, "I quit. You no longer decide for me what's best. I quit." The authority answered back in a condescending tone, "Then who is going to guide you." And I said, "I am. I and my higher guidance." And with that I felt free. When I visualized my path again, there was no valley and I was at my castle. No more waiting to attain my heart's desires. I could experience them right now.

This is when I noticed I had been alone on my journey. My husband and children, family and friends were nowhere to be found. I asked for my path to be made even better and more beneficial for me and to include others with which to share my joy. Immediately, my husband and children were by my side. Roads started appearing from every direction with friends and loved ones coming to visit and cheer me on. It was as if, for the first time, I realized that I did not have to do this alone. I could live the life I wanted and walk the spiritual path with others' support and encouragement. I could have my cake and eat it too. Everyone can. They just need to imagine it that way.

Ironically, when I first began writing this book, I began to feel isolated from my family - nothing horrible, just an awareness that I seemed to be alone a lot. The children would come home from school and do their own thing. My husband would come home from work and go read upstairs while I worked or watched TV in the basement. A few minutes after I had imagined my husband and family by my side at the castle loving and supporting me, my husband came downstairs where I was, sat on the couch and started talking to me. We began having a very engaging, supportive conversation that lasted the rest of the evening. My children have been spending more time with me and have been asking me to do things with them. This is how quickly this process can work. Things can change in a matter of seconds. This is the magic of the 5th dimension at play. I must say playing with it is a lot of fun.

Viewing your path is a key to understanding where you stand in life. Changing your path allows you to find an easier, quicker, and more enjoyable way to get to where you want to go. It is the fastest way to alter your reality.

Here are some other suggestions to help you in sculpting your ideal path.

Ask if your path is an easy or difficult one. Make it easy to get to where you want to be. Put the things you want in reach. Instead of needing to exert effort to go out and get what you want, have it come to you. I remember talking about this with a fellow who wanted to expand his business and bring in more clients. He was viewing this as something that was going to take a lot of time and effort to pull off. I asked him to view it as easy. I asked him to imagine clients just showing up at his office or calling him out of the blue. What if it didn't need to take a lot of effort? I asked if he was able to imagine that possibility. He was and immediately he could feel a shift in his motivation towards attaining his goal. Instead of being hard work that he was not looking forward to, it turned into magical fun wondering how the next client was going to appear.

Notice if your path is prosperous and abundant or if it is barren. Gold coins could line your path, rainbows could be overhead and in the distance, water could be flowing abundantly, trees and flowers growing all around. Make your path lush and vibrant. Dress yourself in robes of gold and deep purple – colors associated with prosperity.

Give your abundance to others and watch how your abundance continues to grow. Feel the overflow of wealth, health, and well-being. Hear laughter and sounds of joy. Look around and feel the gratitude of your path and the joy of walking upon it. Invite friends and family to join you, support, and celebrate with you. Make it as your heart wants it. You cannot be too greedy or selfish. There cannot be too much. If you desire it, honor your desire by allowing its possibility to exist on your path. You are not taking anything away from anyone else's path. They can build their own. Remember, you can't get poor enough to make another person rich just like you can't get sick enough to make another person well. The more wealth and health you pour into your path, the more you show the way for others to do the same with theirs.

Whenever I imagined my path just as I wanted, I would find myself walking alone. This represented a subconscious belief that if I were to truly be me then I would have to be alone. I couldn't be a mom and a wife if I were to walk the path I wanted. When I invited my husband and children to walk with me, they were there, loving and supporting me all the way. Since I have made this change, I have noticed I am more engaged with my family and I feel like it is possible to do and be what I love with the people I love. I never felt this way before.

Do you allow for magic on your path? My youngest daughter described her path as bouncy. When I asked my eldest daughter, aged 8, what her path looked like she described a walkway that changed colors as she walked on it. As she stepped on the brightly colored walkway, lights would appear and unicorns, mermaids, or elephants would spring from the lights. I asked, "So, your path is magical?" and she said, "Yes!"

I knew immediately that my path had lost its magic. For me, it was the missing piece. In my youth, I was fascinated by magic. I loved the idea of sorcery, Merlin, the fairy godmother from Cinderella, and of course Tinker Bell! I have heard it said that a key to understanding your path is to think back to what you wanted to be when you were young. I wanted to be Nadia Comaneci – a Romanian

Olympic gymnast. For those of you who aren't familiar, in the 1976 Olympics, Nadia Comaneci was the first gymnast ever to receive a perfect score in gymnastics. I remember it vividly. I watched her with awe as she finished her perfect dismount from the uneven bars. No one ever expected a perfect ten was even possible in the sport. The scoreboard wasn't even equipped to fully display the perfection. I remember watching in anticipation when the numbers 1.00 came up representing 10.0. I cheered and celebrated her achievement with the rest of the world. Not only did she receive the first perfect 10 in gymnastics that day, but she also went on to receive a total of seven perfect scores during those Olympic games. It was a moment that sticks in my memory. It changed me. I wanted to be her, not because I wanted to be a gymnast, but because I wanted to make possible what was believed to be impossible. I wanted to make magic. I still do. My 8-year-old daughter reminded me of that. Ironically, I was 8 years old when Nadia Comaneci made her magic reminding my soul why it came here.

After talking to my daughter about her magical path, I immediately went into meditation and visualized my path. I gave myself a magic wand and sorcerer's robes like Merlin. I allowed myself to conjure anything I wanted. I also added magical elements like my daughter had done. Unicorns grazed in the distance. Fairies flew and flitted about. Rainbows sparkled in the sky. I also made things look more like a Dr. Seuss book: imaginative, fun, and friendly. Magic was indeed the missing piece. I absolutely loved my path like this. I noticed a difference in my life too. My life seemed to become more magical with wonderful surprises popping up in the most unexpected ways. Magic is the stuff of miracles. I began noticing all sorts of everyday miracles. I was happy. Add magic to your path. You won't regret the feeling of wonder and anticipation that it brings.

Another way to work with your path is to identify what is not going well in your life and then ask to be shown how this is being represented on your path. I wrote this book on my laptop. Because I was spending a great deal of time typing, I began to feel shooting pains down my arm and into my wrist. I asked to be shown how this pain would be illustrated on my path. I saw myself trying to move forward in really thick brush and was caught on a barbed wire fence that I hadn't noticed. I was trying to fight my way free. The Beings of the Light told me to stop fighting, calm down, and take a deep breath. They cleared away the thick brush and dismantled the barbed wire fence. The path was cleared for me to move forward, but whenever I tried to, vines would reach out and grab my feet pulling me back. The Beings of the Light told me I was being held back by my past. When I tried to fight it, it pulled harder. I stopped fighting the vines, sat down, and talked to my past. I told it that I was grateful for all that it taught me, but it was time for me to move forward. I said that in order for me to move forward I needed to leave it behind. I told it I loved it and that it would be well taken care of and that it no longer needed me either. The vines loosened at my feet freeing me to turn around and go forward without feeling the need to look back. The pain in my arm vanished and I no longer had issues typing. This occurred when I was about a quarter into writing my book. The pain never again resurfaced.

The Beings of the Light call this method of visualizing one's path the 3D path. What is behind you represents the past and what is ahead represents the future. It's a linear path, just as time is linear in the 3rd dimension. Wherever you are on the path is the present moment.

The 3D path is a very powerful tool and should not be seen as inferior to 5D methods. In essence you are accessing the 5th dimension with your imagination to change your 3 dimensional world. As you become more comfortable with the notion that you are a multidimensional being, you will likely feel the need to expand your horizons and view the world in a multidimensional way. One way to do this is work with something that The Beings of the Light call the 5D path.

The 5D Path

I must admit when I was first shown the 5 dimensional path, I could barely sit still in it. I found it to be very foreign and uncomfortable, because unlike a 3 dimensional path where you move forward and backward through time in a linear fashion, the 5 dimensional path requires you to sit and be still in the present moment. Stillness is not my biggest strong point, but working with the 5 dimensional path has helped me to find a place of stillness within.

I meditate everyday using the method of guided meditation. I allow my higher guidance to guide my thoughts and visions to where I need to go. This way my mind stays active. I have never been very successful at quieting my mind. Using the method of visualizing me on my 5th dimensional path, I am now realizing the virtues of stillness and am having more success attaining it.

Here is how to view your 5 dimensional path as channeled from The Beings of the Light:

"Imagine a seat cushion that is comfortable and made just for you. Notice its color and shape. Notice its texture. Now sit down on the cushion and find a comfortable posture. Perhaps you cross your legs or sit in a lotus position. No matter how you find yourself upon this cushion, you are comfortable. You are at home.

This seat represents your path in the 5th dimension. From this seat, you are able to view the world from every direction. Notice that as you sit in this seat it is as if you have eyes in the back of your head. You are aware of all your surroundings front and back, side to side, above and below.

When you sit in this seat, the seat of the 5th dimension, you are able to transcend time and space. You are able to view yourself in different situations and in different places.

Unlike your 3D path, where you travel in a linear fashion to move through time, this path allows time to move through you. You are seated in the time of now. All happens in the now. All is now. Your experience of now is based upon where you place your focus.

Notice that in the now, you do not need to venture out to acquire what is wanted. Instead, what is wanted is drawn to you as if you are a magnet. You begin to attract whatever it is you put sustained focus upon. Play with this for a while. Notice that you can attract anything just by thinking of it. The things you attract may find their way to you from any direction, and because you are able to see from every direction in the now, you are not surprised nor blindsided with anything coming your way. You also can no longer turn a blind eye to your own creations. You see them as they happen.

Notice how expansive you feel in the now. You are no longer a physical being, but instead a consciousness. This consciousness knows no limits. It is connected to All That Is, Was, and Will Ever Be, and you are viewing it from a single point of awareness. From this vantage point, put your focus on love and notice what you experience. You may notice that as you breathe love comes in then goes out. With every inhalation love is received and with every exhalation love is given. Then place your focus on lack and notice how you immediately hold your breath. You do not want to exhale because you want to hang on to the love that you have, afraid that if you let it go there will not be any left for you. Fear creates an imbalance by throwing your breathing pattern out of balance. Notice when you breathe in and begin to relax how your focus goes back to love. Play with this. Place your focus on abundance and feel the expansion and the balancing exchange of giving and receiving with your inhalations and exhalations.

Have some fun with your 5D path and begin viewing your world from different vantage points. Ask for your seat cushion to be placed on top of the Eiffel Tower. What do you notice? Ask for your seat to be placed at the depths of the ocean. Notice the difference of perspective. Ask for your seat to be placed in the eyes of another person and view the world from their point of view. Notice how this exercise is useful in breeding compassion. If you can't understand someone or why they are behaving a certain way, place your cushion in their shoes, see from their eyes, feel from their heart and you will understand. This level of understanding and awareness cannot be extracted from your 3D path. It is only in the 5th dimension that true understanding, compassion, and truth is experienced.

If you are unsure of a decision or what direction to take with your life, visit the 5D path. For example, the one you call Fay was unsure how publishing a book would affect her life. We asked her to sit on her 5th dimensional seat and ask to view her world from the eyes of a published author of this book. She immediately felt a sense of calm and gratitude. She noticed doors opening up in every direction for her. She felt love and support, and was surprised by the number of people she touched by sharing her story in writing. This is what she wants. This is what she is creating. As she relaxed into this imagery, her breathing regulated itself and brought her back into balance.

Use this method to give you a sneak preview into what you are creating. If you find you are creating what you don't want, simply ask to be shown the world as if you had created what you did want. Pay attention to what you experience. You don't even have to know what it is that you want. Your heart knows. Your spirit knows. Ask to be transported in time and space to the place where your heart desires to be. If you feel yourself resisting this or find yourself experiencing something unwanted, then this is your mind unwilling to allow the possibility that you can experience your heart's desires. Breathe, and expand into the possibility. Focus on expansion and you will find your way there. Allow yourself to breathe fully and evenly through the resistance and you will find there is nothing to be afraid of. All is well. This is the path to bliss."

As I stated previously, when I first tried to sit on this path, I found it difficult to stay seated on my cushion. I repeatedly wanted to get up and walk toward what I wanted. The Beings of the Light are teaching me to relax and allow what I want to come to me by becoming aware of my breath. This requires no effort but does require focus and trust. They say this is the power of attraction and command. You become a magnet and attract what you focus upon directly to you as if summoning it by magic. You command your world by attracting only what is wanted and retracting all focus on that which is unwanted.

From this point of command, judgment ceases to exist. In your point of experiencing what is wanted, you no longer become fixated on keeping its opposite at bay, thus stopping it from entering your experience. There is no need to make something wrong if you are experiencing what feels right. You cannot feel contraction and expansion at the same time. An example to illustrate this point is to sit on your cushion and transport yourself to the Sea of Wellbeing. While in these waters, there is no illness, therefore, you will be unable to experience illness, because it is simply not present.

The Beings of the Light ask that we play with this new version of our path. It puts our journey into a whole new perspective. However, they say not to abandon the 3D path either. Both are equally important. It is a judgment to say 5 dimensions are better than 3. No one is better or worse, just different. The 3 dimensional experience is a very valued and cherished one from the perspective of the non-physical. It is only in a 3 dimensional world that we can experience a hug, a kiss, or stuff! Imagine never experiencing going from point A to point B in a fast moving car. That is truly a 3 dimensional experience. If we abandoned the 3 dimensional world solely for a 5 dimensional world, we would miss out on all the physicality and tangibility the 3 dimensional world offers. One is not better than the other, just different. For me, it is the use of 5 dimensional magic to create 3 dimensional heaven that makes it all fun.

I have only started to play on this new path and am looking forward to opening up to greater possibilities and new perspectives. The Beings of the Light say to view this path as a playground and a place of exploration. Play, have fun, and enjoy the ride. And above all, remember to breathe.

Applying the Wisdom
The 3D Path

Sit quietly and close your eyes. Ask to see the path you are walking on and then allow your imagination to show you what it is. Notice as many details as you can about your path. How does what you see mirror what you are experiencing in your everyday life?

1. What is your path made of? Make sure it is pleasant to walk on. Add a little bounce!

2. Are you on an easy or difficult journey? Make it easy. Create all the conditions necessary for it to be easy and still have your goals appear.

3. Are there obstacles on your path? Are you free to move forward? Create a clear path for yourself.

4. Who is walking with you? Are you alone? Make sure there is a lot of love and support surrounding you.

5. How much fun is your path? Make it as fun and enjoyable as possible.

6. Are your goals easy to reach or far off in the distance? Make your journey simple and fun.

7. Is your path magical? Allow for miracles to occur along your path. Make yourself the magician.

8. Are you on the right path? Ask to be put on the best and most beneficial path for you and all involved. Notice where you go and what appears.

9. Is your path prosperous and resourceful? Add as many elements or resources as you wish. If you need help, add helpful people along your path. If you need money, line

your path with gold. Use your imagination. When in doubt, ask:

10. "How can I make this better?" and watch what happens.

Visit your path often. Sometimes it takes several visits before the picture you want sticks.

The 5D Path

The Beings of the Light perfectly describe how to view your path from the 5th dimension in this chapter. Follow their instructions and enjoy the stillness and awareness of all directions.

The 5th dimension is a place of magic and is only bound by the limits of your imagination. Go anywhere, be anyone, and enjoy the infinite possibilities. When you trust and allow this method to work for you, your life will have no choice but to change.

CHAPTER 21

✳

Mastering Manifestation

"Everyone thinks of changing the world... but no one thinks of changing himself." – Leo Tolstoy

When I first began learning about spirituality, one of the concepts I came across was the Law of Attraction and understanding the methods to truly creating your life as you want it. I worked very hard at trying to manifest all sorts of things with very little success. I think this is the same for many. People try to make things happen through their thoughts only to find things staying the same or perhaps even getting worse. When this happens, instead of analyzing where they may be going wrong, many people just decide that the idea that we create our life with our thoughts is false and that the Law of Attraction is nothing more than a bunch of mumbo-jumbo. What they don't take time to consider is that we do create with our thoughts, and that perhaps the only reason it hasn't worked in the way they would like is because they aren't aware of the thoughts they are thinking that are creating their results. They truly believe they are thinking positively when they are not.

The Beings of the Light have been instrumental in helping me analyze my thoughts so that I can see how they lead to my present circumstances. I have spent years doing this analysis and have come to the realization that my thoughts, absolutely, in every single case, have created my reality. Certainly it is a tough pill to swallow when you realize that you are the cause of your own suffering. It is much easier to blame that stuff on others. The problem with blame, however, is that it leaves you powerless. In order for your situation to change, the other person has to change. You have no control. The more you put your efforts into controlling other people's behavior, the more you will become frustrated and drained from all the energy you are putting into this powerless situation. If you want results, you need to keep the ball in your court.

There are many books on this subject each explaining the best way to create and manifest what is wanted. I am going to add to the mix giving my best advice as how to make the Law of Attraction work for you. I will also give you several examples so that you can truly begin to realize how your thoughts do indeed create your reality.

Once you take responsibility for your part in the creation that is in front of you, manifestation of what is wanted can occur in three easy steps: defining what is wanted, feeling the way you would feel if the wanted was present, and being grateful for the wonderful manifestation that is coming your way.

Step 1: Take responsibility for your creation and define what you want.

The first thing I do when I realize I am in a situation that I don't want is to admit I created it. I will say to myself, "If I created this, which I did, then I created what I don't want. If this is what I don't want, what is it then that I do want?"

If you are describing your desired outcome in terms of "I don't want it to be like this" or "I don't want it to do that", then you are defining it in terms of what you don't want. You need to focus on the wanted!

It is important to remember to focus on what is wanted in terms of the self. This is the step where people tend to go wrong. They start thinking in terms of how they want other people or things to be instead of how they would like themselves to be. When you keep the focus on you, the creator, you have a much greater chance of success. For example, if my kids are fighting, what do I want? The first thing that comes to mind is that I want them to stop fighting and get along. Notice how I am saying they have to change in order for me to be happy. In this way, I do not involve me in the change. This is a powerless stance. I know, because I have stood in it many times.

What I want to do is decide how I want to feel. When my kids are fighting I feel angry, frustrated, disappointed, and depending on how public the place is, even a little embarrassed that I may not be viewed as a good mother. What I want to feel is content and calm inside, proud of my children, love for my children, and confident that I am a good mother. I want to feel that there is harmony in my world. That is what I want and it all has to do with me. None of this requires them to do anything. This is how I know I am on the right track.

Step 2: Feel the way you would feel if what you want appeared.

People often want to feel awful until their wanted manifestation appears. This is not how it works. The trick is to feel the way you want to feel when the manifestation appears before it appears. This is key in the creation process.

Also, understand it is never enough to just state what you want to manifest. Words are never enough. People often confuse the words they say with the thoughts they think. They are not the same.

A person can say nice words to someone like "You are such a lovely person. I can always rely on you", but be thinking "You're going to let me down just like you always do."

This is another area people have great difficulty mastering – distinguishing their words from their thoughts and feelings. Affirmations only work when you can feel the meaning of the words. In order to get the mind to believe the words, the mind must feel the possibility of those words being true. Wanting the words to be true is not the same as believing in the possibility that they are true. Wanting creates a focus on lack. You want it because it's not there.

Ask yourself, "What thoughts do I need to think in order to feel what I want to feel?" In my example, I want to feel content and calm inside, proud of my children, love for them, that I am a good mother, and that there is harmony in my world. What thoughts then do I need to be thinking to bring out those feelings? I need to think about the times my children made me feel proud and about how much I really do love them. I need to give myself a pat on the back for raising and honoring these two beautiful souls. I need to remind myself that in my heart I know they love each other. When there is harmony in my world, I am thinking thoughts of gratitude and appreciation for all the blessings in my life. My children are wonderful and if they were gone tomorrow, a hole would be left in my heart. That is how much they mean to me. That is how much of a blessing they are to me. When there is harmony in my life, I am NOT thinking how much I wish they'd stop fighting, how ridiculous they are to be fighting, and how angry it makes me that they are. If I thought that, then I would create the feelings those thoughts bring, and I don't want that.

Understand that you can't keep focused on your current reality if you plan to change it. You must focus on a different train of thought and a different feeling. You must accept that you are in an unwanted place, then let go of your displeasure of it so that you can focus upon the pleasure you wish to have in its place. The more you keep focused on your displeasure, the more you will think and feel thoughts that will give displeasure. When you can accept the current situation is not to your liking and let that go to focus on what you do want, change will happen.

In my example of my children fighting, the more I focus on the fact that they are fighting and wrong to be doing so, the more I am prolonging that experience in my reality. The sooner I accept that they are fighting and let go of the notion that it is wrong for them to be doing so, the sooner I can focus on how much I love them and how much I know they love each other. This will create feelings of harmony, which I then will have to, by the Law of Attraction, experience.

Step 3: Thank the forces of creation for working with you and be grateful for the new creation that is coming your way.

And you're done. Go about your business as if everything is just as it should be. When I feel grateful for how wonderful my kids are and how well they get along most of the time, I do not have to worry about the odd squabble nor do I have to be concerned with the one currently in progress, because I know it will be over just as quick as it started.

When we successfully master these steps, we truly are able to create and influence anything in our experience as long as we can imagine it and believe it is possible. When we come to this place of trust, we are then able to create as if by magic. One of the most magical things I have been able to manifest using these three simple steps, and it shocks and humbles me every time I do, is a change in the weather.

Not long after I started my business, I was asked to facilitate a workshop on the topic of shamanism. Shamanism has always been of great interest to me and I even apprenticed under a shaman named Peter Calhoun for a year. While there are many shamanic practices, the ones that resonated most with me were sacred ceremony and commanding the elements. If one could command the elements within then one could command the elements without. In doing so, one can create magic.

The focus of my workshop was to empower each participant to reclaim the powerful shaman they are within. Everyone has the ability to create this magic. It is only doubt in our abilities that keeps us from it.

On the first day of the two-day workshop, I taught them about manifestation and understanding that the thoughts and feelings we have within will manifest the creation without. Shamans are best known for their ability to control the weather. I spoke of how the shaman's role traditionally was to keep balance in the land. If water was needed they called in the rains. When the air needed clearing they called in thunder and lightning. They also were able to call in the winds and bring in the stillness if necessary. The reason most people don't think it's possible to control the weather is because they don't believe they can. Weather, like anything else in our reality, is part of our own creation. When we believe it can be changed, it can. It still requires going through the steps and requirements of manifestation.

Step 1: Define what you want. Remember, if you are describing your desired outcome in terms of "I don't want it to be like this" then you are defining it in terms of what you don't want. In this example, if you want the rain to stop, focusing on the rain stopping is still a focus upon the rain.

Also, define what you want in terms of the self. By saying, "I want the sun to shine." you are not focused on the self. You are focused on needing the weather to change in order for you to be happy. Instead, focus upon how you would feel as if the sun was shining. This is a subtle difference, but enough of one to make the difference between success and disappointment.

Step 2: Feel the manifestation. Understand it will not be enough to say 10,000 times that the sun will shine, if you constantly are thinking, "I can't do this" or "This will never work." or "It's still raining!" Instead, feel your way to your wanted outcome. Feel the warmth of the sun on your skin. Feel the dryness of the ground as you walk upon it in your bare feet. Smell the fragrance of fresh flowers in the air. Taste the cool drink that you poured yourself to enjoy outside in the warm weather. The mind thinks in pictures. Give it the picture you want and feel it!

Step 3: Thank the forces of creation for working with you and be grateful for the new creation that is coming your way. And you're done. If you keep looking out the window and wonder why it hasn't stopped raining yet, then you are shifting your focus back to the rain. If you doubt it's going to stop, and doubt your ability to have some say in the matter, then you will create a result that will allow you to doubt your creative abilities. That result would be continued rain.

This method has worked for me on many occasions. I find I am most successful when I don't care whether it does work or not. The caring about the outcome is similar to needing it to be different. A needy feeling is a feeling of lack. You need it because you don't have it. If you feel the needy feeling, what you want isn't likely coming.

After the first day of the workshop, the lady I was staying with and I went for a walk outside. We could see storm clouds in the distance and they were headed our way. The dark clouds were moving very fast. She said that every time one of these storms came through, the power would go out for long stretches of time. It was very inconvenient. She asked me if I could do anything about it.

I seriously didn't know if I could or not, but I said I'd try. I stood silent for a moment, and just imagined the lights on and the power working. I just imagined things as per usual. Then I said thank you to the forces of creation for co-creating with me, and I left it at that.

We listened to the thunder and felt it shaking the ground as the storm clouds made their way even closer. Then, quite suddenly, they just dissipated. The storm never materialized. I was shocked. Needless to say, the power stayed on as per usual. I said a special thank you to the Universe for making me look good in front of one of my students and for reminding me of how powerful a creator I really am.

I have also worked with the weather spirits while on vacation. I live in Canada where the winters can be long and cold. On a two-week tropical vacation, you really want the weather to be warm and dry. I remember on one vacation in Mexico, the forecast was predicting rain every day. I imagined the feeling of the hot sun and my skin being dry while walking outside. What was interesting is that it did rain quite a bit while we were there, but never when we were outside. Inevitably it would rain when we were inside having lunch or in our room taking an afternoon nap. Our beach and pool time was never spoiled by inclement weather. I remember one day walking out of our room and it was pouring rain. I remember thinking, "Oh well, you can't win them all." As my husband and I finally reached the end of the building that no longer had a roof overhead to keep us dry, the rain stopped suddenly. We never got wet. I just laughed at how perfect things can be. I thanked the weather spirits for keeping us dry and for co-creating this wonderful vacation with me. When we got on the plane to come home, we heard much conversation about how terrible the weather had been. This was not our experience at all. For us, it was fun in the sun!

On another vacation, this time in Punta Cana in the Dominican Republic, the wind was so strong that it was difficult to enjoy ourselves. You couldn't even read a book without your hair whipping into your face or needing to grab items before they blew away. I remember sitting quietly on a sun lounge and getting as quiet and still as I could be. I imagined stillness. I imagined the palms of the trees motionless in the air. I imagined the heat of the sun on my skin. I imagined my hat sitting comfortably and securely on my head. Again, I thanked the forces of creation for this possibility and went about my day in the wind.

The next day, the air was calm. The wind had completely died down. It was wonderful. I said a big thank you as I basked in the sun. The calm stayed the whole time we were on vacation. In fact, towards the end it was getting unbearably hot. I said out loud to the weather spirits, "Would it kill you to give us a little breeze?" The next day the wind had returned granting me my breeze. I smiled once again and said thank you.

I do not share these stories with you to brag or say, "Look how powerful I am." There is still a part of me that doubts my power to create, but I have done this too many times to believe these are mere coincidences. I share these stories with you to remind you of what you are capable of creating and how simple it really is. You just need to focus, feel, and believe.

Once you find your power, avoid the temptation to show it off. The moment you decide to prove to someone you can control the weather is the moment you will find yourself looking like a fool. In the moment that you need something to happen to prove yourself to another, it won't happen. Manifestation is about fulfilling your desires, not about needing them to come true to prove yourself. You need not prove your abilities to anyone. You especially do not need to prove them to yourself. If you need things to be a certain way in order for you to prove to yourself that you are ok, or doing it right, then you are setting yourself up for failure and a feeling of self-hate. You're ok no matter what is going on. You're ok no matter what you have manifested. You do not need to do things in any certain way for you to matter. You matter.

Here are some other examples to help illustrate how our thoughts do create our own reality, and how to successfully change those thoughts to create what is truly wanted.

Scenario 1: I Want Her and I Can't Have Her

I was talking with a friend who wanted to believe in the Law of Attraction, but he had found a loophole he couldn't seem to fill. He asked me to tell him how the Law of Attraction worked with this one scenario: "What if I'm madly in love with someone who is happily married? I can focus on having her in my life all I want, but I'm never going to get her. Therefore, this theory doesn't work."

My response was, "Or does it?"

I continued to explain, "Yes, it is true you create with your thoughts and beliefs. But what you must also realize is that you are not the only creator. In this situation, there is another creator in the situation, and she, through her own thoughts and beliefs, is creating a loving relationship with her partner. Since you believe that she will not leave her husband to be with you, you are creating that very situation. You are focused on what you can't have and, therefore, you can't have it! In this situation, you are focused on lack. You are focused on the fact that you are not in the loving relationship you desire. If you truly loved the person in this scenario, you would wish for them love and happiness. There is no focus on their happiness or even your own. The focus is on your unhappiness of the situation and, therefore, you create more unhappiness for yourself."

What is it that he wants? He wants to feel loved. He wants to feel like he has someone who understands him, someone he desires and who desires him. If my friend truly focused on the possibility of finding a love like that with someone who was free to give him that love in return, then he would immediately shift the focus of his thoughts. If he became grateful for the possibility of that person actually existing, and grateful for the love, understanding, and desire he has to give, he would start feeling differently about himself. If he kept his focus on these feelings of gratitude, the woman of his dreams would have no choice but to appear. If she doesn't, it isn't because the Law of Attraction doesn't work. It would be because he didn't maintain his focus on what he wanted and began to doubt the possibility of this actually happening, thus creating the experience that allows him to doubt the process. Or perhaps he was impatient and began noticing that she wasn't there yet, thus creating the experience of her not being there.

What's interesting about this scenario is that it outlines the one crucial mistake we humans often make when we don't take full responsibility for our creations. The mistake is he needs someone else to change in order for him to get what he wants. This is a futile and frustrating strategy. Sure on the surface, it looks easy enough. If only she would leave her husband so that he could be with her. The reality is he could wait a lifetime for her to leave her spouse. It may never happen. Even if it did, there's no guarantee she would choose to be with him. Either way, he ends up alone, all because he waited for that person to change.

The key is to create what you want without interfering in anyone else's creative process. That does not mean you must do this all alone. Instead, you will find those who want to create with you for their benefit coming into your life. The fact that they want to create with you is of benefit to you, too. Win win. Mutually beneficial. It can be very easy. Start putting parameters on the creation like – it has to be this person and no one else - and you limit the ease of the solution or lose it altogether.

The last thing to point out is that in this scenario, my friend is not willing to accept that someone else who is a better fit for him may be out there. He also is unwilling to let go of the belief that his friend is wrong to be with her husband. If he would focus on the feelings of love, desire, and companionship coming into his life, instead of seeing how they are absent, he would be in love sooner than he thinks.

Scenario 2: My Spouse is Making Me Angry

While on vacation in Hawaii, my husband was having trouble settling in and relaxing. He became grumpy and irritable. I, in my deep state of compassion, had decided he was just being a jerk. He would complain about little things. He seemed very angry and any little thing would just set him off. This, in turn, made me angry and I began blaming him for ruining our family vacation. If only he would just get in a better mood, I thought, so that we could all be happy!

One night, just as we were settling down to go to sleep, he yelled at our daughters for something really insignificant (I'd tell you what it was but I don't remember anymore). I was so annoyed that he was upsetting the girls needlessly, and acting like a tyrant. I remember thinking, and possibly even saying, some nasty thoughts just to let him know how I felt. It doesn't take a rocket scientist to realize that he did not stop, laugh, and say, "Of course. How silly of me to be acting this way. What was I thinking?" Tensions were running high, but luckily we stopped ourselves from saying anything further.

As things quieted down and we were in our beds, I painfully acknowledged that I was creating this tension in my experience and it was the exact opposite of what I wanted. I then asked myself, "What do I want? If this is the opposite of what I want, then what is it that I do want?"

I was almost in tears as I realized I was incredibly far away from feeling what I wanted. I wanted us to be happy, carefree, and jovial. I wanted us to laugh together and enjoy each other's company. I wanted to feel appreciated and loved by him. I wanted these things not only for me, but for him too, because I really love him.

I then realized my thoughts about my husband had not been kind, loving, or appreciating. They were downright nasty. Thoughts create reality and my nasty thoughts were in full creative force. It took a bit of pride swallowing, but I forced myself to change them. It took effort, but I forced myself to remember times when my husband was loving and appreciative of me. I forced myself to remember the many times when he had been a loving father, relaxed, and happy to be in our presence. I pictured us all together in a family hug, smiling, without a care in the world. Whenever the thoughts of "but he is being such a jerk" crept in, I would stomp them out with a new thought of "that is what I don't want. I'm creating what I do want and what I do want is for us all to be happy and kind to each other. Calling him a jerk is neither kind nor a way to make him happy. I believe his mood is temporary, and I wish him love and care so that he can let go of what is troubling him. I believe in the possibility of our happy family and I am very grateful for it."

I must admit this was not an easy process for me. I was very angry with my husband. I realized that in order for my thoughts to change to what I wanted, I had to let go of the anger I was harboring and feel the love I have for him in my heart. As I held the feeling of gratitude for having such a loving husband, all relaxed within me. All previous behavior was forgiven. I went to sleep feeling relieved. I woke up with my new creation. From that morning on, all his anger, grumpiness, and complaints had been replaced with smiles and contentment. My husband had seemingly changed overnight. But I knew the truth. What really happened was that I changed overnight, thus changing my experience.

One of the biggest obstacles to our creating what we want is blame. As long as we are blaming someone else for our reality, we will not be free of it. Notice how the act of blaming someone else for your misery does not provide a solution. It only provides you with a stubborn righteousness about how wrong the other person is. When you focus on how wrong something or someone is, you will get more of it. When I told my husband in anger that he was being a jerk, he became even angrier. It's not until I softened my feelings about him that he softened.

The other obstacle to creating what we want is wishing something from someone else, but not providing it in return. In this case, I wanted to feel loved and appreciated by my husband, but I was in no way feeling love for or appreciating him. As soon as I did, my circumstances changed. This, for me, can be the most difficult thing, because it really does require that one change his mind. Notice the difference from feeling unloved and unappreciated to feeling loved and appreciated. In order to truly feel each, you must focus upon it and give up all awareness of the opposite. When I focused solely on my loving feelings for my husband, I created loving feelings in return. This is manifestation.

Scenario 3: I'm Being Bullied and It's Not My Fault

You're right. It's not your fault, but, like everything else in your experience, it is your creation. The toughest pill to swallow is that you or someone you love has created a situation of victimization. It is much easier to place blame upon the bully for the entire creation. It stands to reason that if there were no bullies, there would be no victims. But the truth works the other way as well. If there were no victims, there would be no bullies.

"If only they (the bullies) would change, then I wouldn't have to be a victim any longer." Do you see all the ways victims keep themselves trapped in victimization with this way of thinking? They are caught up in the blame and this leaves them unable to let go of it so that they can focus on what is really wanted – to feel and be treated with respect.

I in no way advocate bullying. I do know, however, that fully blaming the bully is not a solution. When the victim can take ownership for their creation, they have power. Power is something that victims do not have. The minute you have power, you cease to be a victim.

I was bullied in elementary school from kindergarten until about Grade Eight. I never fit in well with the other kids and became the brunt of their jokes. I was often called ugly and stupid, even though my looks were fine and I was a straight A student. I wasn't the biggest girl in my class, but I was strong having been raised on a farm and had done my fair share of chores. Even though I was strong physically, I was weak emotionally. Whenever the popular kids started to insult me, I would shut down my emotions and try to become invisible. I never wanted them to see how much I was letting their words hurt me. On occasion, I would try to insult them back, but this would just end up in them laughing at me and telling me how wrong I was. Again, I would retreat.

When I looked back on the situation, understanding that my thoughts create my reality, I understood completely how I created this role of victimization. The thoughts I had of myself were less than complimentary. The kids didn't like me because I didn't like myself. I was always finding fault and pointing out what was wrong with me, instead of acknowledging what was right with me. The other kids around me reflected those thoughts back to me like a mirror by telling me I was ugly, wrong, and stupid. I also used to complain that the kids were always picking on me. This became a self-fulfilling prophecy. My thoughts of the bullies were very nasty as well. I thought they were mean and cruel, and that became my experience. I never stopped to appreciate myself for my good qualities, nor did I stop to appreciate them for their good qualities. In my mind, they didn't have any. And that is what I experienced. That is what I created.

As long as I made the bullies the ones in the wrong, I never had to address the hurtful thoughts I had of myself. The only problem was, as long as they were to blame, I didn't have any power to make it stop.

I found my way out of victimization by standing up for myself. I was on the playground at noon hour minding my own business. I was playing with a softball that one of the bullies wanted and I wouldn't give it to her. She did her best to insult and threaten me in order for me to give her the ball, but I wouldn't give in. Something just snapped inside me that said "Enough." I wasn't going to let her manipulate me anymore. I didn't want to fight. I remember staying uncharacteristically calm through it all. For once, I had the upper hand. She had no power over me because, for the first time, I didn't give it to her. You could say I kept the ball in my court (no pun intended). I didn't hide. I didn't buckle. I didn't stoop to giving threats or hurling insults. I just stayed completely focused on standing my ground at any cost. When she realized that I wasn't backing down, she gave in and left. This was the last day I was bullied. No one ever bothered me again.

What changed? Me. More specifically, my thoughts changed. I stopped thinking she had power over me and that I was powerless. I found the confidence to stand my ground for what was right for me and I won. She won too. She no longer needed to bully me. Instead, she saw me as someone whose confidence was not going to be wavered. Why did she see that? Because I felt it. I created a way out of victimization through my thoughts that spilled their way over into my actions.

What's interesting to me is that this altercation I had with her was quite private. No one else witnessed what went on between us. Neither one of us said anything to anyone. Yet, everyone stopped bullying me from that day forward. Why? Because I gained confidence and took back my personal power and worth. When I ceased being a victim in my own mind, I ceased being a victim to others. I attracted no more bullies.

I have deep compassion for those who have been victimized, but my compassion will not stop it. Victims must find their own way out of victimization. The thoughts and beliefs surrounding victimization is that the victim is powerless to stop what is happening to them. If you are a victim, notice how needing someone to change or be present to protect you at every moment, still keeps you a victim. As you realize you are the creator of your life and that you, through a series of thoughts and beliefs about yourself and this situation, created this situation, you can now create its opposite. I realize that even if that girl did decide to stop bullying me on her own, another bully would have found their way to me until I changed the thoughts I was thinking. I had to change. It's just like someone who gets out of one abusive relationship and finds themselves smack dab in the middle of another one. It's because their thoughts about how they deserve to be treated or how others always treat them have not changed. It is not until they change their thoughts that they stop the cycle.

If you are being bullied or abused, I have the deepest compassion for you. I know first hand the deep emotional pain being a victim creates. Please know I am not blaming you for your situation. Blame never provides a solution. You do, however, have the power to pull yourself out of your situation.

The first thing to do is to realize the past has happened and there is no point spending energy wishing it could have been different. It is what it is – the past. Your aim is to create a different situation starting now. It is time to start focusing on what it is you want.

Cease the need to blame yourself or another for what has happened. Forgive them and forgive yourself for all that has transpired. This is not to say you approve. It just says you will no longer allow them or you to stop yourself from moving forward.

Realize that any emotion you have around this situation whether it be hate, jealousy, anger, rage, insecurity, inferiority, or all of the above, was not given to you but resides within you. Because you are the owner of these emotions, you are fully capable of letting them go. Use the letting go method as described in Chapter 12 to free yourself from the pain.

Imagine what it is you really want to feel. Be careful not to imagine what you do not want. For example, "I want them to stop being mean to me" still focuses on them being mean to you. Instead change it to, "I want to be treated with kindness." Feel what it would be like if you were treated with kindness. Feel what it would be like if you were kind to yourself. Most victims have a very low view of themselves. It is time to imagine you as someone who deserves to be treated with kindness and make yourself the first one to offer it.

Also, be aware of the need to gain acceptance or approval from your bully. You do not need them to like you. It's their choice what they think of you and you are not able to change that. The girl who bullied me did not ever end up being my friend. She did, however, treat me with respect as I did her. When you change, the bully will either change their mind about you and treat you well, or they may disappear and avoid you altogether. They may even continue to throw insults your way, but now they won't bother you. In any case, you end up feeling confident and accepting of yourself.

NOTE: My example uses two young girls on a playground. Even if our situation had escalated, it would have resulted in nothing more than a few scratches or bruises. If you are in a potentially dangerous situation, remove yourself from any possibility of confrontation. Do not put yourself in danger. Do all the creative changing in private using the methods I describe above. Seek help, and know you must still do the inner work to truly change your situation. Never waver from the belief that you can create something better for yourself, even if it takes you several tries to make a small shift. You're new at this. Give yourself room to practice. Keep telling yourself, "I can do this." Every time you find yourself back in similar circumstances, keep saying to yourself, "This is what I do not want. What is it that I want?" And focus on the new images and feelings. Never, ever give up. Victims give up. You no longer can call yourself a victim. You are a powerful creator learning to create a new possibility for yourself. And you will succeed. No one else can change your mind for you. You must do it. And you can. You are. You will. Believe in the possibility of succeeding. Believe in yourself. And above all, love yourself no matter what.

Using Your Emotions to Guide You

One day I became very angry at my husband for not helping me clean the house. Then, I was angry with myself for being angry, because a spiritual person is supposed to be positive and full of joy. Then, I was angry with my husband again for making me angry and allowing me to get away from my good natured self.

One of the mistakes I have made on my spiritual journey is to try to never feel negative emotions. Whenever I felt a negative emotion, I felt like I was failing or that I shouldn't be feeling the emotion. "Masters of spirituality surely never feel negative emotions. I must be doing something wrong," I thought. Making myself wrong led to more negative emotions such as guilt, blame, judgment, and frustration.

The Beings of the Light guided me through this letting me know all my emotions were valid and helpful indicators to the present state of my thoughts. They said, "If you feel angry, accept you feel angry. It is your resistance to your acceptance of your feelings that causes you to remain disconnected from your Source of Well-being. You feel like you are doing something wrong which in turn allows you to berate yourself for not doing it right. What if your anger was doing it right?"

"But something is wrong. I don't want to feel angry." I replied.

"Then the feeling of anger is letting you know that you are thinking thoughts that are creating an unwanted situation. The anger is a divine messenger. Don't shoot the messenger!"

Don't shoot the messenger. The phrase rang in my ears loud and clear. The messenger, in this case, the anger, was letting me know that I was focusing my thoughts on something unwanted. Since I didn't like the message, I wanted to destroy it. I especially didn't like the message that implied I should change my way of thinking. This is when the stubbornness of my ego flared up and said, "No, I'm not changing. Why should I? My husband should be the one to change. If he doesn't, I'm going to remain angry."

Notice how this thinking leaves me in a state of powerlessness. I may believe my power is in standing my ground, but by doing so, I leave myself without a solution. I remain angry. The true power is in the ability to accept one's emotions, be grateful for the message they are relaying, and move towards the solution by changing the thinking that caused the emotions in the first place.

How do you actually do this? What is the practical application? Here are the steps that The Beings of the Light laid out for me. I analyze my example of being angry with my husband using these steps in italics.

1. Notice the unwanted feeling. *I am angry with my husband.*

2. Accept that this is a message sent in love. The feeling is a message, much like the Check Engine light in your car. It is an indicator that my thoughts have veered off the path of wantedness and need addressing. *I don't want my house to be messy. I don't want to feel angry. Message: You are thinking thoughts that are creating what you do not want.*

3. Be honest with yourself. What are the true feelings you are experiencing? When we allow ourselves to truly identify our feelings, we find that they generally run much deeper than we would first like to admit. Often hurt and rejection is covered up by anger. Being angry with someone is easier to deal with than the actual hurt and rejection one is feeling. Jealousy is another emotion that is covered up with anger or sometimes indifference. Insecurity is often covered up with blame. If you make someone else wrong, then maybe no one will notice

your own weaknesses. Most of us have spent our lives not aware of our true feelings. Instead, we cover them up or stuff them away and ignore them, hoping they will disappear. The truth is, the feeling just becomes deposited somewhere in the body. If you stuff the feeling enough times, that spot in the body will begin to hurt or malfunction. In order to release the pain or restore function, the feelings stuffed in that area must be addressed. The truth must come out. This is the acceptance part of the process. When you accept that the feeling is present, and no longer deny its existence, you no longer keep yourself victim to it. *I feel angry. Underneath the anger, I feel unappreciated and unloved. I want help. I am scared that no one loves me enough to help me.*

4. Let the feeling go. In order for this to happen, you must love yourself enough to allow your feelings of blame and righteousness to be replaced with feelings of love and acceptance. In your act of hating or blaming another, you will never be able to feel the love you deserve. You will never be able to accept that every person has a right to his own opinion, just as you have a right to yours. You do not need to wait for the other person to change, apologize, or love you in order for you to feel love and acceptance. You have the power to do that on your own. *I wanted my husband to fill the void of these feelings. His not wanting to clean the house didn't mean he didn't love me. It just meant he didn't feel like cleaning up. When I take a moment to appreciate and love myself for all the work that I do to make our house a home, I feel better. I knew I wanted help, but didn't ask for it. I only jumped to the conclusion that my husband wouldn't help me, which allowed me to get angry and blame him. When I calm down, and think about all the work my husband does do, all my anger goes away.*

Note: When people finally come to a place of letting go, they will feel an emotional release, often in the form of tears.

Other signs of release are sighs, yawning, nausea, diahorrea, cold sweats, or even frequent urination. This is the body's way of getting rid of the toxic elements that you have been holding onto. Welcome these symptoms, because it means that you are releasing. Breathe throughout the process and it will make the process go more smoothly. While some of these letting go symptoms may seem undesirable, the opposite is worse. Hanging onto toxic thoughts and energy will continue to plague you with pain, discomfort, and perhaps even illness. After the release is complete, you will feel much better. Most people report feeling lighter, rejuvenated, and calm.

Would You Rather Be Right or Happy?

When I was working in the corporate world, a situation arose where the steps I just outlined became very helpful to me. Without them, I would not be where I am today.

I was working at a university in a supervisory position. My manager and I got along very well. One summer, my manager went on vacation for 6 weeks. I filled in for him in his absence. From that point on, I often would be asked to fill in whenever he was away. I became familiar with many of his duties and felt I could effectively manage the department.

When the director of our unit, my manager's manager, took a new job in Human Resources, my manager was asked to fill her position for up to six months to a year, so that a proper nationwide search could be done to fill the position. My manager accepted this temporary posting, leaving his job vacant. The university posted this temporary position and I applied for it. I felt quite confident I would be the successful candidate given I had proven myself in the role and already had a strong, respectful relationship with the staff.

In the end, it came down to two candidates: me and another man from outside the department. I was extremely happy with my interview and knew I couldn't have answered the questions any better than I had. I was very excited about this new opportunity. Not only was it a promotion, meaning a higher salary and more responsibility, but also was a validation of the good work I brought to our department.

To make a long story short, I didn't get the job. I was devastated. I felt like all my credibility had been taken away. Why else would they hire an outside person over me? The most disappointing factor in all this was the person who made the final decision in the hiring was my manager. This is what bothered me the most. He had picked someone else over me. My devastation turned to anger. Actually, it was more like rage. Inside, I was furious. I think I chose to be furious, because the hurt and rejection I was feeling underneath felt much worse than the anger.

The more I went over in my mind how my manager had made the wrong decision and that I clearly was the right person for the job, the more angry and upset I became. Many of the staff came up to me trying to console me. They told me they wished I had gotten the job. This just fuelled my righteousness – even the staff thought I should be the manager! But none of it made me feel better. The more reasons I thought of to prove I was right about this situation and that my manager was wrong, the worse I felt.

For the next week, my emotions plummeted into a dark spiral of depression. I lost all my motivation to do my job. I didn't want to interact with anyone. I didn't want to be at work at all. Knowing what I know about spirituality, I knew I couldn't go on like this. I could feel this killing my spirit. I prayed for help. The Beings of the Light led me through the steps.

They asked me to notice all the feelings I was having. I was angry, but underneath the anger I was hurt. I felt rejected. I felt embarrassed that I didn't get the job. I felt shame for not being enough to be chosen for the position. When I became honest with my feelings, I realized that I was really being very hard on myself.

Next, they asked me to accept that the past cannot be undone. I had been going over in my mind the interview, my performance, trying to figure out what I should have said or done to make this different. The Beings of the Light pointed out to me that this was just another way for me to keep my thoughts focused on the fact that I believed I wasn't enough. It was time to accept I did an excellent job in the interview and as a supervisor. If I was lacking in an area, I could not go back and change it. I could only change moving forward.

The other part of this for me to accept was that the decision to hire someone else was in the past and could not be changed. No one was going to reverse the decision. Even if the successful candidate backed out, I knew I wouldn't want to fill the position anymore. I didn't want to be there.

I had to admit, just by accepting the truth of the situation, I was already beginning to feel better.

The next step was the hardest and the most important. It was time to let go. I had to let go of being right. The more right I made myself, the worse I felt. The more wrong I made my manager, the more hate I felt in my heart for him. Deep down, I knew I really liked and appreciated this man. I didn't want to hate him. I just didn't know how else to not feel hurt by him.

The Beings of the Light asked me to consider that he wasn't wrong. In my mind, if he wasn't wrong, then I must be incompetent. They then asked me to consider that I am competent and that he still wasn't wrong. If that was the case, then this whole scenario was to get me to hate my job, because I certainly didn't want to be there anymore. Then, I was asked to consider that perhaps it was time for me to move on and this provided the push I needed to get out of my comfort zone.

I knew the truth of the words as soon as I heard them. I had wanted to go into business for myself for a long time. I just didn't know how to do it. I let go of my being right and allowed myself to believe in the possibility that this was a blessing in disguise. I allowed myself the opportunity to believe that I would have made an excellent manager. I also let go of my righteousness allowing my manager his right to make decisions, even if I didn't agree with them.

My motivation returned, but this time it was aimed at me moving forward. In less than a month, a series of events presented themselves that led me out of my position at the university to ultimately me starting my own business and following my dream. I now have the deepest gratitude for my manager and the decision he made. If he had chosen me as the successful candidate for the job, I may have never left the university to fulfill my heart's desires. Now, it appears to me that it was the best decision he ever made.

What I learned from this is that you cannot be right in a way that makes another person wrong, and be happy at the same time. In order to be happy, you have to allow yourself your own opinion and allow everyone else the right to theirs, even if their opinion is the total opposite to what you think. Making someone wrong is the key to unhappiness. Whenever we need others to think or act a certain way in order for us to be happy, we place ourselves in a powerless position. When we let go of the notion that others are the cause of our misery, and ask how to come to a place of joy or peace, we allow ourselves to find the strength and resources that are always available in infinite abundance within.

I worked with a client who was very frustrated with a co-worker. The co-worker would always find fault with her work and this made my client very unhappy. She worked extra hard to ensure the accuracy and efficiency of her work to no avail. She didn't know what to do to please this person. Her co-worker's negativity was making her feel unhappy at a job she otherwise very much enjoyed.

What my client was doing was needing someone else to be happy in order for her to be happy. I asked my client if she was happy with her work. She said she was. I asked if she was willing to accept that it was her right to be happy with her work and that it was her co-worker's right to be unhappy with it. A light bulb went on for my client. She had never considered the possibility that she had a right to think and feel one way while others felt and thought the opposite. This was immensely freeing. She began enjoying her work again despite her co-worker's negative outlook. It no longer affected her, because she no longer was using her co-worker as a means to validate her worth.

Often our misery is held in our belief that others have to validate our worth. It is only the self that has to validate our worth. Once that is done, everyone else's opinion is insignificant. The moment you need another to validate you, you open yourself up to ridicule. It is like you are telling your soul, "You are only ok if I find a bunch of people who think that you are. Then maybe, just maybe, I'll think you're ok too." Instead, tell your soul, "I believe you are ok. I love you. The others out there may not, but that's only because they are not allowing me the right to my opinion. I allow my right to my opinion, just as I allow them the right to theirs." And that, more than anything else, is the key to happiness.

Manifesting what we want is a tricky business. Understanding that we are the creator of our life and co-creating with others who are the creators of their lives, we come into a place of empowerment and self-realization. Understanding that our emotions are messengers that tell us what direction our thoughts are headed is the key to fully taking control of our life's direction. Keeping the focus on our ability to change instead of on the need to have others change around us allows us the ability to steer our own ship. Life is about taking our power back. In order to do that, we must stop giving it away to others and take full responsibility for our own creations. It is time to accept that we have the right and ability to create whatever we choose, while accepting that others around us have the right and ability to create whatever they choose, even if their choice is opposite to ours. When we cease looking at what the other guy is doing and pay attention solely to what we are doing, then we have the makings of a happy life.

Applying the Wisdom
When Wishing to Manifest Something:

1. Take responsibility for your creation and define what you want. Say "If I created this, which I did, then I created what I don't want. If this is what I don't want, what is it then that I do want?"

2. Feel the way you would feel if the wanted manifestation has appeared. Ask, "What thoughts do I need to think in order to feel what I want to feel?" and think them. Create pictures in your mind as if what you want has happened. Remember, it is

not that you need to make what you want happen. Instead, you are accepting that the possibility of what you want exists by allowing the possibility to be experienced first in the mind.

3. Be grateful for the wonderful things and experiences you are creating. Rejoice and celebrate in the knowing they can and do exist, and are on their way!

Using Your Emotions as Messengers

1. Notice the unwanted feeling.

2. Accept that the unwanted feeling is a message sent in love and indicates that your thoughts have veered off the path of what is wanted.

3. Be honest with yourself. What are the true feelings you are experiencing? What is underneath the feelings on the surface? Admit the truth and acknowledge the presence of the unwanted feelings.

4. Let the feelings go by releasing righteousness and blame. Stop making anyone wrong just because you don't agree with them. Decide what you want to feel and feel it regardless of what anyone else thinks.

CHAPTER 22

Pet Peeve

"The cat is the mirror of his human's mind… the dog is the mirror of his human's physical appearance." – Winifred Carriere

A client of mine came to me quite distraught over the behavior of her cats. They were urinating in various places in the house for no apparent reason. She said she had tried everything, and was at her wits end. She was hoping I could help.

I actually had never read animal energy before and wasn't sure I would be able to do anything. I said I'd give it a try and asked The Beings of the Light to guide me. I immediately began to receive information regarding the issue.

The first information I received was that pets often represent what is going on unexpressed within oneself. In this case, I was being shown that the cats were expressing the feelings of her youngest son. Urine is always a sign of unexpressed anger. As I tuned into her son's energy, I could feel his anger and frustration. I could tell he felt he was being punished for something that wasn't his fault. He felt like the world was against him and he was helpless to do anything about it. I asked her if she knew of any reason why her youngest son may be feeling this way.

She said it all made sense. She and her son's father no longer were in a relationship and there were unresolved issues regarding custody. She also knew that her son was very unhappy because he was no longer able to spend as much time at his dad's, which was the place where he was allowed to play his favorite pastime, video games. She did not have video games in her home because she didn't like the violence that was portrayed in them.

The angels showed me that he felt like his mom didn't trust him and that he was being unfairly punished for the fact his parents were no longer together. He felt like all the things that brought him joy were being denied him. Since he was unable to voice his anger and resentment, the cats were doing it for him.

They also showed me that the video games were not as damaging to him as she was imagining. They showed me that they were a release for his frustrations. I was also shown that when we deny our children the things they love out of fear, we are doing them a disservice. Fear is never a beneficial place from which to act. Acting from fear creates negative outcomes. Acting from love creates positive outcomes. For example, keeping a child from going near a busy street can be an act of love or an act of fear. If you act from love, the child will likely stay away from the street. If you act from fear, the child will resent you for denying its freedom and will run towards the street the moment you turn your back.

I told her the information I was getting. I told her that I knew she didn't approve of video games, but was there any way to allow him some access to play at home so that he doesn't feel like he is being punished. She told me he was asking for a game app for his Ipad.

I told her that it may be a great idea to surprise him with the app as a gift just for him. I told her to make sure not to say he was getting it because he had done some chores or needed to do something to earn it. She was to give it to him just because she loved him. In this way, she could feel good in the giving and he would feel good in the receiving.

That night I received an email message from her saying thank you in capital letters. She said her son was really very surprised when she presented him with his gift and that she hadn't seen him this happy in such a long time. She said she even heard him say under his breath, "and I got this just for being me." It brought tears to my eyes.

I emailed her back a couple of days later and asked her about the cats. She said they had stopped urinating outside their litter box the night she gave her son the Ipad app. I thanked The Beings of the Light for their divine guidance and for the grace that had been bestowed on my client's family. Once again, I was shown that love heals.

Applying the Wisdom

If your pet is behaving out of character, pay attention to the parallels in your emotional life or the lives of those living in the house. When you resolve your issues, they will resolve theirs. Understand, however, that our pets do not have a life span as long as ours. Often their decision to cross over is a sign for us to let go of attachments, and understand that to everything there is a season.

As a parent, if you find yourself fighting constantly with your child over an issue, you may wish to ask yourself whether you are denying them out of your fear for them. Ask for guidance to allow your child to live and be as they like while keeping them safe. When you deny children their freedom they will rebel. When you allow them freedom with loving guidance, they may make mistakes, but they will learn. They will also feel comfortable coming to you for help when they do make those mistakes. This is the communication you want. When you trust them, they will want to make you proud. Give them a safe place to fall and a loving environment to express themselves.

CHAPTER 23

✳

When Dreams Become Reality

"If you don't have a dream, how are you going to make a dream come true?" – Oscar Hammerstein

When my husband and I were first married, we bought a quaint bungalow in a nice neighborhood in the city. While we loved this home, we dreamed of someday living on an acreage, just outside the city. We wanted to be close enough to the city that we didn't feel isolated, but far enough away that we could feel the benefits of country life. A five to ten minute drive to the city limits would be ideal.

One day while at the drug store, my husband noticed a book of house plans. He bought the magazine and brought it home saying that maybe we should go through it and see if there were any homes that we liked. Perhaps we might find the plan of our future dream home that we could build on the acreage that we planned to own in the future. We decided to look through the book separately. My husband was to pick out his favorite house from the magazine and I was to pick out mine. This would give us an idea of what each other wanted in a dream home.

To our surprise, we both picked the same house. We cut the pages from the magazine that contained the pictures, floor plans, and ordering information for the architectural blueprints, and pasted them into a journal that we would keep. This became our new dream - to build and live in this house on an acreage just east of the city in which we lived. We also added that we wanted the landscape to be beautiful with rolling hills. Of course, we knew this dream was somewhere down the road because we both were just starting out and had very little money.

Fast-forward twelve years. We are living in the same house in the same neighborhood in the city. We have our two beautiful daughters and are much more established in our careers. On one particular beautiful autumn day, I was sitting in my back yard. I was sitting very quietly and it was one of those moments when everything goes still and it's just you and the sun and the fresh air. At that moment, I heard a very loud message in my head say, "Prepare your house for sale."

This voice jolted me out of my place of serene stillness. I looked at my house and knew it would be less than a year left living in it. We had no plans to move, but I just knew it was coming. I thanked my house for being a wonderful starter home for us, and a safe and loving place for our two children to explore.

In the next few months, I painted and prepped. My husband thought I was crazy when I started taking the kitchen cupboards off their hinges. I told him I was going to sand and paint them and that it was time to paint the kitchen too. Our kitchen was dated and certainly needed a lift. My husband said we should just think about renovating the next summer instead of going through the hassle of painting. I told him there wasn't time for that.

In the spring, an acquaintance of mine was selling her acreage and offering it to people she knew before she put it on the market. I showed my husband the email she sent, and he agreed it wouldn't hurt to go look at it. I was also intrigued because a few years earlier, a shaman had told me we would get our acreage from someone who honored the land and wished the next owners of their property to do the same. This certainly fit that description.

We went to look at the property, and while it was lovely, we knew it wasn't for us. The house was the same square footage as our house in the city and we wanted something larger. It also was a little further from the city than we wanted to be. While we said no to this opportunity, we decided to look at other listings to see what else was out there.

We viewed a few properties, none that seemed to fit what we wanted. We went back to our journal and the plans of our original dream home. My husband said that maybe it was time to start looking for a lot of land with rolling hills close to the city and build our house. I said, "Wouldn't it be nice if we could find that lot with our house already built on it?" He laughed, but I was serious. The idea of building a house from scratch seemed like a lot of stress and headache.

A few weeks later, I was getting my car serviced at a local garage. While I was waiting for them to finish, I picked up a real-estate flyer of local house listings and began flipping through. My jaw dropped as I happened upon a listing I had never noticed before. I was staring at a listing that featured a house on an acreage that looked the same as the picture of the house my husband and I pulled out of the house plans magazine twelve years earlier.

I brought the flyer home and showed my husband. I told him, "I think I found our house."

Of course, there were some factors to consider. The house was outside of our price range by about $30,000. This is why we hadn't come across it before now. It didn't fall into the search parameters we were using on the Internet. The other thing is we had no idea where it was located. If it were far out of the city or in a direction that we didn't want (we wanted east), it wouldn't be right for us. We hired a realtor and decided to go ahead and view it anyway.

To our surprise, the house was literally a 5-minute drive east of the city limits. The lot that the house sat on was beautiful with rolling hills, mature trees, and the entire property was completely landscaped. We wanted at least 5 acres of land and this was 7. The house was beautiful. It was as if it had been built just for us. And the cherry on top of this delicious treat was that the list price of the property dropped $35,000 the day we viewed it, because it had been on the market for over 6 months. Sold!

It was a fairy tale come true. Our house sold in less than a week and we were moved out and into our new home in less than 2 months. I guess the shaman was right after all. If my friend hadn't been selling her acreage we probably wouldn't have started looking at listings when we did. In a round about way, we did get our dream home because of her.

When I look at our house, I remind myself that dreams do come true when you truly believe. I am very glad that we never closed off our vision of living in this home. It would have been very easy many times for us to say it was likely never going to happen. We never did that. We just kept believing that someday, when the time was right, this place would find us. And it did.

I love the fact that I am living back in nature, and feeling the freedom of wide-open space. Nature is very healing. What I wasn't expecting was this Nature needing healing from me. It seems there was an even greater reason why we moved to this place – one that has made me realize more deeply the interconnectedness of all living things.

Hearing the Cries of the Land

Not long after we moved to our new acreage, I began to feel uneasy with my surroundings. My daughters, who are very perceptive, wouldn't go in the basement without one of us with them. My youngest daughter told me she didn't want to play on the outdoor swing set because she felt like someone was going to push her off. When I lay in my bed and imagined the energy of our property, there seemed to be a darkness to it. It wasn't a cloud hovering over it, but more of a darkness that came from the ground up. I called upon The Beings of the Light and the angels to come clear the darkness and guide me in any way I could be of help.

This awareness started me on the journey of working with the land. While I understood Mother Earth had a living energy to her, I had always found her energy to be full of light. I had never really considered the land could be damaged.

Because this was all new to me, I called upon a feng shui consultant who was also well versed in land clearing. She pinpointed three very large negative vortexes that intersected the house. Through intent and the laying of copper rods and crystals, we were able to neutralize and close the negative vortexes. After we did that, my children felt much happier being in the basement.

While we were closing off the largest negative vortex, I began receiving images of what occurred on this land from times past. I was shown the aboriginal peoples of this land in war with the white man. I saw the native women being raped and the loss of the sacred feminine as the soldiers overpowered and defiled them in front of their husbands and sons. I saw a massive amount of bloodshed. I could feel a deep sadness and pain in the heart of the land. It was as if the blood that spilled upon this land carried the emotion of the people that perished here. The rain has not been able to wash away its pain and suffering. It has remained, stuck in the memory of the land itself.

I could see the effects of this negative energy in nature. There were pockets of trees that were dead, not only on our property, but all around the area. I felt the sadness, torture, and pain most severely in these deadwood areas.

I knew I had been brought to this land to help heal it. Closing the negative vortexes helped, but there was still much more to do. I asked for guidance and followed it the best I could.

The first thing I did was take a bag of clear quartz crystal points, with the intent of making a healing crystal grid around my property. Every ten feet or so, I placed a crystal in the ground around the property's perimeter. When I was done, I probably had laid about 150 crystals in the land. I also placed crystal points around my children's play set with the intent that a space for safe play, fun, enjoyment, laughter, and innocence be created.

Next, I spent time sitting at one of the deadwood areas. I told the land that it was time to release the past and feel the joy of life once again. What surprised me was that I felt compelled to sing, something that if you heard me do in a karaoke bar you would ask me to stop. As I opened my mouth, a series of melodic vowel sounds came out. I just sang whatever came to me. The song sounded ancient and I knew it was providing a vibration of healing for the land and a memory of joyful times past for the souls that still lingered there in the pain.

I hung Tibetan prayer flags that I had bought on a trip my husband and I took to Tibet a few years earlier, and strung them from one dead tree to another with the intent that they bring blessings to this area and all the land. I left tobacco as an offering and burned sage and sweetgrass to purify the land and thank it for being the soil I called home. I asked the land to remember its original innocence and to forgive what had happened upon it. I asked it to replace the pain with peace.

I have some friends who are much better versed in land practices and when I asked them for help, they showed me a few other techniques that have proven to be very helpful.

The first is to imagine anchoring a large crystal deep into the land, so large that it can emanate energy for miles in every direction. This helps clear any blocks or negativity from the land on a continual basis. The land graciously accepted the crystal. Then we called upon the Master Soul of the Land. It seemed that the care of this property was still held energetically with the previous owners. I made a plea to the Master Soul of the Land to give me and my family the key to this land where we agreed to care for it and nurture it to the best of our ability. The Master Soul agreed and gave us the key. For the first time, I felt like this really was my home and was accepted by the land.

A few months later, I was guided to buy a drum similar to the drums played at First Nations ceremonies. A friend attuned my drum to reiki so that when I played it, it would send out healing energy with its sound. I walked around the property playing the drum, sending the healing energy wherever I went.

I then began to realize that the land was healing, but the souls attached to the land were not. It seemed that the souls who lost their lives on this land were still here, or perhaps just fragments of their souls. In any case, I could feel their presence and their desperation. I could feel their sadness and worry for the future generations. They were worried for the children.

I tried to assure them that the slaughter was over and the children were safe, but they didn't trust me. Unsure of what to do, I called upon the Archangels to assist these souls back into the light. I could sense their reluctance to go until they were satisfied that the children would be safe. As far as I was concerned, it was out of my hands. I left it in the hands of the angels.

Shortly after that, I began to be visited in my waking moments each morning by a Native American goddess named White Buffalo Calf Woman. At first, she would just appear and smile at me, then disappear. I had no idea what she wanted, but I sensed it had something to do with the connection to the land. Finally, one morning she appeared, but instead of disappearing, she handed me a peace pipe. It was long and thin, feathers of eagle and hawk hung from one side. It was made of wood but glowed pure white. I asked her what I was supposed to do with it. "Make peace." was all she said and then disappeared again. This happened again and again until I realized she must mean for me to make peace with myself. This happened while I was writing this book. I surmised she was helping me gain the courage to speak my truth.

I did some research about who White Buffalo Calf Woman is. She is a prophet who appeared to the Lakotas offering a peace pipe that would give power to their prayers and strengthen their connection between heaven and earth. When she left them, she turned into a buffalo of many colors signifying the unity of all races and the truth that we are all One. It is believed that she will mark her return with the birth of a white buffalo calf. I don't know if a white buffalo calf has been born, but I feel like her presence is close by. Her presence is certainly apparent to me.

Her visits didn't stop. She has let me know that she wants all races to come together as one and to forgive all mistakes and transgressions of the past. She told me that in order to do this, the souls that still linger in the land must forgive and become one once again with the Creator, the Light. As long as these souls stay, the land cannot be healed. If the land cannot be healed, those connected to the land cannot be healed. They will carry the burden of the past around with them, passing it on from generation to generation. She then showed me how this has happened with our First Nations people. As long as they carry the burden of the pain of the past with them, they will never find the freedom and the peace they seek. In order for this to happen, there must be forgiveness. We all must see that we are not separate. We are One. When one of our brothers is in pain, then we all are, regardless of race and creed.

I was shown how when one is in pain, how badly they wish for the one who caused it to feel their pain. She showed me how we think that this will bring justice and even the score, but in truth it only perpetuates the suffering. Hate begets hate. Pain begets pain. Love begets love. It is the only way.

She showed me that when these souls who linger in the land realize this truth, they will gladly go home to the light. When they do, the generations on Earth who have been carrying the weight of their ancestors around with them, will be free to choose a new path.

I knew I was being given an opportunity to expedite the healing of our First Nations people. I was honored and at the same time confused. Why me? I'm considered a white woman.

White Buffalo Calf Woman spoke to me. "You are a white woman and a rainbow woman. You, like all humans, carry the colors of all who went before you and all who shall come after you. You understand this. Many do not. Your soul has lived lives as a First Nations person who was slain by the white man. Your soul has already forgiven. The souls lingering in the land have not. It is time for them to see that we are all One. They will see you for who you are – one of them and one of those they oppose. They will see that you have lived through the pain to which they cling, and found the way past it. This is why I have passed the peace pipe to you to carry. Offer it to the souls that linger in the land. When they see you carry the pipe, they will know. They will trust."

This was a lot to take in. It seemed like too important and too big of task for me to do. I asked why she just didn't show them the way and offer them the pipe herself. She answered, "The forgiveness has to be granted and accepted on the earthly plane. Do not be afraid. You are not the only human I have passed the peace pipe to. You are one of many on the earthly plane who have been called."

Like all assignments I have agreed to take on in the name of the light, this one was relatively easy. I knew that Spirit never asked more of you than you were willing or able to give. If all I had to do was go into meditation and call forth the souls that lingered in this land, show them a peace pipe, and ask that they be guided home, I could do that. I wanted to do that, because the happier my land is, the happier my kids are, my family is, and I am.

It was time to fulfill my promise. I grabbed my drum and went outside. I found a comfortable spot to sit under a tree in my back yard. I wasn't sure what was going to happen. Since I had never really called forth a bunch of unforgiving souls before, I felt it prudent to surround myself with white light. As I was doing this, I noticed White Buffalo Calf Woman standing behind me. I knew instantly that I would be safe and that she had my back.

I began to drum. I settled into a rhythmical beat, closed my eyes, and mentally asked the souls lingering in the land to come forth. At this moment, something odd happened. I began to notice myself sitting in various parts of the land drumming away, doing the same thing I was doing under my tree. It was as if I had been cloned thousands of times over and each clone sat on a patch of grass about 50 yards apart in a diamond-grid like fashion. I was told that this process was happening multidimensionally, in more than one time and space simultaneously.

I proceeded with the process. Souls of the natives, who had lived and perished here before me, lined up to receive the peace pipe that I offered them. Our eyes would meet, and when they did I saw the light of forgiveness and understanding in them. Then, they would move to the side and stand under a portal of light that transported them home to a place of peace. I was able to see the same thing happening with all of my multidimensional clones as well.

Close to the end of my line, stood a very large native man. He had great anger in his eyes. When it came his turn, I offered him the peace pipe. He took the pipe, broke it in two, and threw it to the ground. I could feel his pain. I understood. I walked over to the pipe and picked up the pieces. They immediately mended themselves and became whole. Now holding the perfectly intact pipe, I once again offered it to him. This time he took it gently, as if understanding that love can never be broken. He handed it back to me with gratitude in his eyes, and allowed himself to be transported home to a place of peace. I was moved.

The line ended, but I knew we weren't done. Just then, I began drumming a different beat. I closed my eyes once again and was surprised by what I saw. Souls of the white man began lining up to be blessed by the peace pipe. They held their heads down in shame for what they had done. They, too, needed forgiveness.

I looked down and saw that I was wearing calfskin robes. I had changed into my Native American self. Each white man that came forth had pain in his eyes, but it was a different kind of pain. It was shame. They didn't know how to be forgiven. They didn't know how to forgive themselves. As they graciously accepted the peace pipe blessing, they were able to let go of their shame and come to a place of acceptance within themselves. They then proceeded to the portal of light where a Native American soul was standing to take them by the hand and welcome them home. It was beautiful.

I recognized one of the white men standing in the line. I knew he had raped me and my daughters in a previous lifetime. I offered him the peace pipe and I could see remorse in his eyes. I forgave him and he forgave himself. This is the power of the peace pipe. I took his hand and walked him to the portal welcoming him home.

Then something miraculous happened. I noticed the souls were no longer standing in line. Instead, the souls of the natives and the souls of the white man were finding each other, embracing, and going home together. They no longer needed my assistance. They were doing it on their own. White Buffalo Calf Woman told me that our work was done here and that I could now go inside. The healing had begun.

I know this story may sound unbelievable to many, but it is true. It is perhaps one of the most precious moments I have experienced on this magical, spiritual journey. It has given me the understanding that with love anything is possible. It showed me how the hurts and pains of the past can and will be healed, and that someday, although it still may be sometime far in the future, we will see each other as One, not separate entities who need to take sides against one another. I see now that there will be peace.

Applying the Wisdom

Whether you have recently moved into a home or not, it is always a good idea to go inside your mind and ask the Master Soul of the Land to give you the key to your property. Let the Master Soul know you are there to honor, respect, and love the land you occupy and are open to suggestions of how you can improve it.

Also, you can add love to your land by using your imagination to anchor in a crystal of love into its center. The crystal is very large and looks like a boulder. Thank the land and ask it to remember its original perfection. Be grateful for it, because it gives you the space on which you live. You can do this even if you are living on concrete or in an apartment building. There is earth underneath. Bless it and be kind to it, and it will bless everything that lies above it in return.

If you would like an assignment to be of divine service, then ask for one. When I first began my spiritual journey, one of my first assignments was to pick up litter, especially plastic, if I came across it. Another one asked me to compost and recycle. Another was to start using cleaning products that were green and void of chemicals. Taking care of the Earth is a very important assignment. When we take care of her, we take care of us. My next big assignment was to acknowledge the water and ask it to remember its original programming of perfection. It was a very easy assignment; it just required a commitment to take the few seconds it took to do.

Assignments are generally simple and easy, but will make a profound impact even if you can't see it. Do not let your ego get in the way of your assignment and say, "That's too simple. I want something more challenging." Start simple and life gets simpler. It is through the assignments that I am becoming more aware and gaining a greater understanding of how easy and simple it is to make a profound impact. The offering of the peace pipe to souls took about ten to fifteen minutes, was easy and fun, and extremely powerful. It really is time to break the belief that in order for something to work it has to be hard. I have come to find, the simpler the process, the more powerful the process. The easier it gets, the easier it gets!

Ask for an assignment and have the courage to do what is being offered. It will make a profound impact on your life and the lives of others, even if you cannot readily see how. Trust.

CHAPTER 24

Breathing Pattern Adjustment

"Fear is excitement without the breath." – Dr. Fritz Perls

As I have mentioned previously, at various times while writing this book I have encountered anxiety. The anxiety varied from worry over whether I would have enough material to fill a book, to whether the book would be published, to how people would react if it did get published. All this anxiety stemmed from my fears of admitting the truth of who I am, how I live, and what I believe.

As I came closer to finishing this book, the anxiety became more intense. On one particular night, I couldn't sleep and could feel the fear welling up inside me wondering how my immediate family might react to this book. Since I couldn't seem to get my mind off the subject, I got out of bed and went downstairs. Whenever I am in these dark feelings, I do what I always do – make a silent plea to the universe by saying "Help me!" then sit quietly waiting for a response.

My plea did not go unnoticed. I immediately felt a warm energy surround me. I recognized this energy as I had encountered it before. It was not the energy of The Beings of the Light, although I could tell they were present. It was the energy of a group of high beings known as the Galactic Council. I knew from experience that when the Galactic Council shows up, something good and transformational is going to happen.

The Galactic Council is a group of highly advanced light beings that are in divine service to Earth and humanity assisting in our evolution. They appear to those who are ready to serve in the evolutionary process. If you are wishing to assist in divine service with the Galactic Council, you only need ask. If your request is of pure heart and when you are ready, you will feel their presence and be given blessing and divine guidance as how to proceed. As is true with all divine service, you are never given more than you can handle. You are never asked to do anything you are unwilling to do. You always have the choice to decline any guidance or request without judgment or consequence. The energy of the Galactic Council is one of unconditional love and support.

I remember my first encounter with the Galactic Council was at a meditation circle. My friend and mentor, Bonnie Bogner, was leading a DNA activation process facilitated by this high council. The DNA activation process is one of awakening the DNA in our body to a higher vibration so that it can evolve into a system that is more crystalline-based instead of carbon-based. This evolutionary process is slowly occurring in all humans. By consciously receiving the DNA activation from the Galactic Council, it enables the evolutionary process to quicken and take root within the collective consciousness.

The reason our DNA is becoming more crystalline in structure is so that we are physically able to carry more light on Earth. In order for us to hold and carry the amount of light that we wish to grow into, we need a physical vehicle (the human body) that is capable of holding the light. By adapting our DNA, we will be able to be light in physical form. Without this evolutionary shift, our bodies would literally burn up and we would ascend as spirit (which means we would die). With the evolutionary shift, we can now stay alive on Earth as human and live as spirit.

After the DNA activation, I asked my friend if I could facilitate this process for others. She told me if I receive the information from the Galactic Council, I could. She explained that she is not doing the activation, but is channeling their energy. At the time, I did not feel I was ready to do this and I left it at that.

A few months later I found out that another friend of mine was channeling the energy of the Galactic Council and doing DNA activations for her clients. This gave me the confidence to ask to be granted this ability. At my next workshop, which was my first Spirituality for Beginners workshop, I was planning to do a basic chakra clearing meditation. To my surprise, the Galactic Council showed up. I channeled their energy and the participants received the DNA activation and chakra clearing at once. This has remained part of the class ever since.

The next time the Galactic Council showed up in my life was at one of our Energy Spa Days. They assisted us in receiving a prosperity attunement. It was an immensely powerful attuning of our energies to release all belief in lack and tap into the infinite abundance that the Universe has to offer. The prosperity energy was brought into our hands signifying the balance between giving and receiving. It also solidified the wisdom and understanding that the only payment required for receiving abundance is gratitude. It was literally only a few days after receiving this attunement that I began writing this book. I was finally able to accept the belief that I had something to say and receive the words in which to say it.

And now, once again, I was in the presence of the Galactic Council. I didn't know what blessing was in store for me, but I knew it was going to help me. I thanked them for coming and began to tell them my fears. They stopped me from going any further and told me to stop focusing on my fears and to just relax and breathe. I gratefully obeyed their request.

As I did so, they let me know that they were providing me with a Breathing Pattern Adjustment. They said that I had picked up non-beneficial breathing patterns from my youth, and it was time for me to allow more oxygen through each breath, and also to breathe in a more consistent pattern. They explained that in times of stress, I had a tendency to hold my breath. This intensified the anxiety I felt, because it blocked the flow of energy or divine inspiration that the breath provides.

As I relaxed, I could feel my breathing deepen and my diaphragm loosen. The tension in my shoulders that I had grown accustomed to began to melt. It was as if restrictive chains were being lifted off my chest and back. I could feel my lungs fill fully with each inhale and empty fully with each exhale. My breathing slowed, evened, and deepened. The anxiety was gone.

I thanked the Galactic Council for their divine grace. I was told that this was another method I could incorporate in one of my workshops. All I needed to do was channel their energy and they would adjust each person as needed. They explained to me that this is also a necessary step in our evolutionary process. Most people have not mastered optimal breathing patterns.

They also told me that they were going to adjust me in stages. They said I needn't worry nor did I need to do anything. When the time was right they would appear again to perform the next adjustment. I would need eight adjustments in total to get me to an optimal breathing pattern and that this would occur over the next year. I was also told that if I wanted to expedite the process that I could set my intent for it to happen sooner. It was up to me.

I immediately set my intent for this process to occur in the fastest time frame possible that would provide me with grace and ease. I didn't want to overwhelm myself with anxiety in order to get there. I felt that by just setting the intent, that the process would take approximately 6 months to complete instead of just over a year.

The Galactic Council wrapped me in loving energy and bid me goodnight. I went back to bed feeling content, fell asleep quickly and slept soundly until morning.

Applying the Wisdom

Ask the Galactic Council for your own breathing pattern adjustment. Sit quietly and pay attention to your breathing. You will instinctively know when the process is complete. If you are unable to relax or feel the comfort and ease of this process, you likely are not ready or willing to receive it at this time. Ask for whatever is necessary to happen in order to allow you to be ready to receive and that this be done with grace and ease for your highest benefit and the benefit of all involved.

If you feel called or interested in divine service, ask for it. One of the reasons the Galactic Council asked me to write about my experiences with them is to let others know they exist and welcome anyone who wishes to aid in the evolutionary process of the planet. My work with them has brought me tremendous blessings and insights. It is always an honor when they make their presence known. Only goodness is carried within their being.

CHAPTER 25

✳

Gratitude and Appreciation

"Be thankful for what you have; you'll end up having more. If you concentrate on what you don't have, you will never, ever have enough." - Oprah Winfrey

When I'm feeling anxious or worried, I am often directed to focus upon the things for which I am grateful. The Beings of the Light say gratitude and appreciation are the highest and best feelings one can experience. When one appreciates, one loves unconditionally.

I used to have trouble bringing forth true feelings of gratitude. As I grew up, I felt like I was living without much of the time. I spent far more time feeling like I didn't have enough than feeling grateful for what I had. For those who still feel this way, I understand. I know what it is like to want and feel like you are being left without. A friend and mentor helped me over this hurdle by asking me one simple question.

What would you miss tomorrow if it were gone today? An indication of what you are truly grateful for, and for what truly adds value to your life is in the answer to this question.

I asked myself the question and began making the ever so long list of answers. The obvious came up first. I would certainly miss my children and my husband. I would miss my siblings and my dad. All my friends – ok I get it. I would miss the people of the world – those I had met and not yet met – that have helped me and will help me on my journey. Thank you. Thank you. Thank you. I could really feel a new appreciation for them as I pondered the idea of them being gone.

Next, I realized I would miss all the things in Nature. I would miss the flowers, the trees, grass, sunshine, stars, the moon, air, the sky, the ground, rocks, rivers, lakes, and oceans, the wind, thunder and lightning, snow, rain, plants, the sunrise, the sunset, rainbows, animals, ladybugs…the list goes on. I began to understand the value of these things. I felt the appreciation and deep gratitude for them and for the Earth herself.

What really surprised me was how much I would miss the stuff. We often take stuff for granted, but really the stuff adds a great deal of value to our physical experience. It gives us much for which to be grateful. I would miss chairs, sofas, bathtubs, indoor plumbing, electricity, pillows, my bed, blankets, and food, especially chocolate. I would miss airplanes, hotels, cars, highways, stores, toys, clothes, hot tubs, swimming pools, cups, plates, cutlery, shampoo – you get the picture. The list is infinite. This is because the universe is infinite and everything in it adds value. There is always something to appreciate in everything, even if it is not readily apparent.

Imagine if there were no doorknobs? There's something one can easily take for granted until they're gone and we're stuck climbing through windows or keeping the doors open letting in the cold or the bugs. They serve a purpose. When we find purpose in people and things, we give them value. When we value something, this is a form of appreciation. In other words, it is a form of love. Best of all, it feels good.

The Beings of the Light have shown me that whatever value we place on the things in our outer experience is equal to the value we place on ourselves in our inner experience. This is why it is detrimental to take things for granted. Thinking something is no big deal is the same as telling yourself you're no big deal. Finding no value in a person or thing is the same as finding no value in yourself.

You may think a piece of paper is no big deal, a dime a dozen. But imagine if there was no paper left in all the world. You may think differently about that same piece of paper if it suddenly appeared. You may find it to be priceless. Therefore, paper is valuable and deserves appreciation. When you take time to appreciate the little things in life, it is the same as appreciating yourself. It is also the safest way to express love, because a piece of paper would never reject you. It would accept you for who you are without judgment.

I have never been grossly overweight and am considered to be a thin person. Despite this fact, I have always struggled with body image. What I have come to notice is it really doesn't matter how pretty or skinny a person is, everyone can have insecurities about their body and find ways to devalue it.

Recently, I gained 10 pounds. I was very unhappy about this. I watched the weight increase day by day (it took a few months). The reason I was able to do this is because I weigh myself every morning. I have found this to be a way to not let my weight get away with me. I don't recommend it for everyone, but it is a strategy that works for me.

Upon reflection, I found that when I gained the first three pounds, I was very upset. I would get on the scale and be upset that my weight was higher than I wanted it to be. I stayed at that weight for sometime, each day wishing I were three pounds lighter. Then it turned into 4 pounds, then 5 pounds heavier. It didn't seem to matter what I ate or didn't eat; the pounds remained. By the time I had gained ten pounds and said enough was enough, I had already been feeding myself with so much disdain that I felt unhappy and defeated. When I looked in the mirror I saw a protruding tummy, which I hated, and fat on my back, which thickened my waist. I didn't like it at all.

The Beings of the Light pointed out to me that my weight gain had nothing to do with food and everything to do with ungratefulness. They reminded me that the most important answer to the gratitude question of "What would I miss tomorrow if it were gone today?" was myself. If I weren't there, wouldn't I miss me? If my body were gone, wouldn't I miss it? In this way, one can begin to appreciate how very important the body is to us. Indeed, it is what makes the Light Being a human.

They asked me what I hated about my body. I said I hated my current weight and my protruding belly. I let them know that I would not miss them if they were gone tomorrow. They laughed and said, "Oh really? You wouldn't miss your current weight if it completely disappeared tomorrow? And what if you woke up tomorrow and your current weight was 20 pounds heavier? Wouldn't you wish you were your current weight once again?" I hadn't thought of it like that before. When I thought about it, I would be very grateful to go back to the weight that was only 3 pounds higher than my regular weight, especially now that I was 10 pounds heavier. It really is relative.

The Beings of the Light told me that when you can appreciate your current weight and truly love where you are at, you will move towards where you wish to go. One way to appreciate my current weight is to view it in relation to a weight much larger than mine. Regarding the stomach issue, I knew I would miss my stomach, protruding or not, if it were completely gone. In this context, it is incredibly valuable. The same goes for one's flabby arms or thunder thighs. They certainly would take on new meaning if you found them amputated in the middle of the night. I bet you'd take those flabby arms back in a second and love them deeply given the only other option was to have them completely removed.

When we cease to hate what we want to change and appreciate what we have, we have a much better chance of inducing wanted change. The appreciation is a form of love. When we feel love for ourselves, we will create a more loving outcome.

I heard of an experiment where a woman took a group of overweight people and asked them to eat whatever they wanted. All they needed to do was tell their body they loved it and find ways to appreciate themselves. After a short time, most of the group had lost ten pounds. When I began appreciating myself and my body, my weight reduced, I felt better, and I didn't do a thing to change my diet.

When my mom died, I truly began to feel a true appreciation for life, love, and family. I was experiencing the gratitude question in reality. What would I miss? My mom!

My mom had a massive heart attack at home. Through the determination and stamina of my brother and paramedics, they were able to get her heart to start beating again, long enough to get her to the hospital and stabilized with drugs and machines to assist her in her breathing. After a couple of days, we realized that she wasn't going to recover consciousness as her organs were beginning to shut down. The blessing in this is that each one of my brothers and sisters were given the opportunity to say goodbye to our mom before she died.

As I sat by her bedside holding her hand, I knew I needed to use this time to say everything that I had left unsaid. All I could think of to say was, "I love you. I love you so much. I'm sorry if I ever hurt you. I didn't mean it, because I love you so much." That's all that there is to say in the end. If that is the case, then I guess that is all there is to say in the beginning and the middle. Love is all that matters. Everything else is a distraction, an excuse to avoid the truth – love is all there ever is and ever was.

With my mom I felt pure unconditional appreciation for who she was and what she had done for me, and I knew I was going to miss it. I experienced something very profound that day, a feeling of gratitude I had never felt before in my life. I felt gratitude for the preciousness of life.

As my husband drove me and our children back home from the hospital, I realized that all the things I complained about were simply unimportant. I hated it when my kids fought, but I knew in that moment that the opportunity to hear them fight was something precious. If they were gone, I would never be able to experience them in all their humanness again. If they were gone, I would give anything to hear them fighting because that would mean they were back.

I try to remember this whenever I get annoyed or upset at someone or something. I remind myself of me with my mom, and I instantly become grateful for the opportunity to experience the annoyance and the choice to love. That brings me joy. Love always leads to a feeling of well-being. It is the answer to every question and the solution to every problem.

I encourage you not to wait until it's too late to take inventory of all the blessings you have and opportunities to love that you may be wasting. If you do not feel joy in your heart, perhaps it is because your focus is on the stuff that doesn't really matter – the stuff that would be forgiven in a heartbeat if you found that person was dying at your feet or if you found yourself dying at theirs. Perhaps it's because you have forgotten to remind yourself of the value that someone holds within your life. Above all, appreciate your ability to love and appreciate. If that were gone tomorrow, you surely would miss it.

Applying the Wisdom

Take inventory of all the things in your life that are valuable to you by asking yourself the gratitude question: What would you miss tomorrow if it were gone today? Whenever you feel as if something is lacking in your life, refer to this question and really feel how grateful you are for the things that are in your life.

If you are still unable to shake the feelings of lack, understand that saying thank you and feeling gratitude are two different things. Words without feeling are empty. Unless you can truly feel the value for what you are saying thank you for, you will never come to a place of joy, love, or appreciation.

Afterword: The Journey Continues

"Focus on the journey, not the destination. Joy is found not in finishing an activity but in doing it." - Greg Anderson

I've done it. I have scratched another item off my bucket list. I have managed to write a book. When I look back on the journey, I am amazed at how easy and hard, fun and frustrating the entire process was.

I remember when I was relentlessly asking what I should write my book about. The Beings of the Light quietly and humbly said, "You could write a book about us." My answer at the time was, "No bloody way!" I wasn't ready to expose myself to the world as I was. I was scared. I was scared to admit what I loved, what I believed, and who I was, even to myself.

The Beings of the Light never pushed or made demands. Spirit never does. They simply opened doors and planted seeds as to how I could explain my story in a safe and helpful way. They made me see when I mentioned their existence to other people how those people felt more whole and at home. It is my hope that, in some way, this book has done that for you.

The more I acknowledge The Beings of the Light in my life, the more my spirit comes alive. The more I open to the wonder and the mystery, the more magic appears in my life, the more joy I feel, and the more risks I take. I have been led to the realization that the seemingly impossible is nothing more than illusion, and the real truth is everything and anything has the chance to exist simply by our willingness to imagine, believe, and trust in the process.

The subconscious mind is a magical playground that I have had the pleasure to explore, navigate, and witness. I have come to appreciate its complexity and perfection, and the depth of its wisdom and infinite potential to create new and better worlds for us all, when only we have the courage to face what it remembers.

The subconscious mind holds all the reasons, all the meanings we have put to every instance, every interaction, and every moment we have ever experienced. It is a beautiful book of our entire self, heart and soul. When we allow ourselves to read that book with honest eyes and then give ourselves permission to rewrite the parts we dare to experience differently, we can change our world. We just have to be willing to face what's really there, open the closets and let the skeletons out, and accept that whatever is there, is there for a reason. When the reason no longer fits, we can choose a new meaning, one that ends the suffering and heals the hurts of the past. This is the beauty of life; nothing is permanent.

Sometimes it's not that simple. Sometimes we have to feel the pain, acknowledge its presence, and admit that we are often cowards to tell the truth. Sometimes, it is only in feeling the pain that we find the reason to choose differently. In this way, pain brings the great gift of perspective, for it is often only in knowing the difference that we appreciate anything. How can we appreciate love if we have not felt hate? How can we appreciate beauty when we have not witnessed the ugly? How can we feel the freedom of acceptance until we have felt the restrictiveness of judgment? It is in the 3 dimensional world of polarity that we are able to truly understand what love is by understanding what it is not. It is in the 5th dimensional world of infinity that we transcend the polarity and free ourselves of our judgments, our restrictions, and rules. It is the one place where all exists and all is perfect, no matter how light or dark it is. In the 5th dimension, it all has purpose, value, and a reason. There is no need to fight against anything. There is only the need to flow with what is and enjoy the ride in the only moment that exists – now.

I have reached a milestone on my journey by completing this book, but my journey is far from over. Like the horizon, that can be viewed from the distance but never reached, so it is with life. Part of the journey is to make and reach goals, but you never reach the end of the road. There is always another step to take, always another moment to experience. Even in death, I believe, the journey continues as we explore the world of the non-physical as spirit, and contemplate our next steps for our soul's growth from what we have experienced on Earth.

As I journey forward on this spiritual path, I know I will continue to uncover past hurts to heal and fears to face. I know I will enjoy moments of magic, passion, love, and anticipation. I look forward to experiencing the untold wonders that lay before me, the blessings of the hardships I have yet to face, and the miracles that will occur to keep me straight on my path of faith and discovery. I will continue to climb towards and reach my heart's desires, making new ones along the way.

I thank you for walking with me for this piece of my journey and being open to the idea that there is much more to us and this world than what is readily apparent at first glance. I hope that this tiny glimpse into my experience has allowed you to view and experience your own life in a new way. I hope that it has prompted you to question your beliefs, not because you need to change them, but because it is in the questioning that we receive all our answers. It is my wish for every person to realize the passion and purpose of their soul and the power each one of us holds within to make our heart's desires a reality.

Now, as I write the final words of what is to be this book, I am humbled and grateful by the beautiful journey creating it has taken me on, saddened that it's over, and like the mother who watches their child leave home to find their own way, hopeful for what this book may become. No matter what happens, I am happy to have found the courage to share my knowledge of the existence of The Beings of the Light and the wisdom of Azez with you. May you find the magic that dwells in the depths of your beautiful subconscious mind, the courage to make the seemingly impossible possible, and a deep gratitude for the wonderful light that you are. Don't be afraid to shine that light, for it is why you came here. Without it lit, the world is a darker place.

Like the perfect vacation that you wish would never end, this is how I feel about this book. Perhaps that is why I am having such difficulty writing the last sentence – I don't want this leg of my journey to end. But end it must. And now, another door opens. I step inside and see where it takes me…

About the Author

Fay Thompson is a licensed Spiritual Health Coach specializing in Subconscious Mind Correction, a spiritual teacher, and channel. She offers private healing sessions, facilitates various workshops, and also is an accomplished inspirational speaker. Her aim is to empower each person to stand in their truth and realize the immense potential within. For more information on Fay and her work, visit www.faythompson.com.